LEADERS GUIDE

UNSHAKABLE
FAITH

Living Strong in the Kingdom of God

DEBRA L. BUTTERFIELD

CrossRiver

ST. JOSEPH, MISSOURI USA

For more on Debra L. Butterfield, please visit — DebraLButterfield.com

Cover image: Copyright Michaelliu888888 | Dreamstime.com
https://www.dreamstime.com/michaelliu888888_info
Cover design by Tamara Clymer

Printed in the United States

FOREWORD

This book contains valuable information for those who want to know more about spiritual warfare—to know where the weapons of our warfare lie and to pick them up and start fighting the fight. It is not for the beginner only, but also for those who are more mature in the faith.

The author has gone from a Christian with no power to a Spirit-filled Christian that is right in the middle of the fight for "The Faith of the Cross." Her book is for everyone who wants to know the ministry in the form of victory.

God has not called Spirit-filled Christians to be idle, but to fight as violent men and women of prayer, who not only know Him (Jesus) as His bride, or child, but as a soldier standing ready for battle.

Pastor Larry Gray
Founder & President
Hosanna International Ministries

CONTENTS

I have set the Lord continually before me;
Because He is at my right hand, I will not be shaken.
Psalm 16:8 NASB

I know the Lord is always with me.
I will not be shaken, for he is right beside me.
Psalm 16:8 NLT

How to Use This Study

Welcome! I'm so glad you've chosen to do this Bible study. My heartfelt desire is to see you grow as a Christian, but also to grow deeper in your relationship with God. This study is designed to help you do both.

Each lesson has been designed to be completed within fifteen to twenty minutes. Some chapters have five days of lessons, others have six days because the topic was too lengthy to cover in five.

Do not feel you need to do one lesson per day. Complete this study in whatever time frame is convenient for you.

This book can be used as an individual study or done as a group. This leader's guide has been designed to offer options. Your group could meet once a week and discuss one chapter per week or dive deeper and take two weeks per chapter. These time lines are offered only as a guide. You'll find all the leader questions at the end of the book.

Goals of this Study
- Teach you the fundamentals of Christianity
- Grow your faith
- Grow your relationship with God

- Help you stand strong in your belief in God and His promises.

Materials Needed

The primary tool you will need to complete this study is a Bible. If you don't have a printed copy, you can access many digital versions of the Bible on BlueLetterBible.org, BibleGateway .com, or via phone apps like Bible by Life Church, and The Bible app from YouVersion.

Occasionally, you'll need a dictionary.

You can write your answers directly in the book or in a journal of your own.

Group Study

Individual study books of *Unshakable Faith* can be purchased at a discount with orders of five (5) or more, shipped to one place. Available to US residents only. Contact deb@crossriver-media.com to order.

PART ONE:

KINGDOM BASIC TRAINING

INTRODUCTION

Yeah, right, you're thinking. Unshakable faith is impossible. As I prayed about what to title this Bible study, I had the same reaction when those words paraded through my thoughts. But God was right there with His answer, "Everything is possible with God."

And that's the key—we are doing life *with* God. Seeking first His Kingdom, His vision and plan for our lives, and His guidance in fulfilling that vision. Rather than doing things in our own power or through our own knowledge and skills, we seek the wisdom and guidance of Holy Spirit first and foremost.

If you think you should never feel fear or discouragement or any other negative emotion, that's wrong thinking. We are emotional beings; it's natural to experience negative emotions as well as positive. This doesn't mean your faith has been shaken.

You will be shaken only when you embrace that negative emotion and focus on the circumstances. In the pages that follow, you will learn the fundamentals of the Christian faith and how to apply God's Word, the Bible, to your life. This study will give you the tools to resist Satan and conquer the difficulties and trials he assaults you with. You will learn how to stand your ground and fight back with the Word of God.

Having unshakable faith doesn't happen overnight. Nor does it happen without commitment to knowing God's Word and developing your relationship with Him. If you are looking for a quick, easy fix, you might as well return this book or give it to a friend.

Unshakable faith will come as you keep your focus on God's promises and then, like David, you can say,

"I have set the Lord continually before me; Because He is at my right hand, I will not be shaken" (Psalm 16:8).

There are three videos that accompany this Bible study. The introductory video is to be viewed at your first meeting and introduces part 1. It also includes information that is not in the study.

The next video introduces part 2. Watch it prior to beginning your discussion of the first lesson of part 2. The third video expounds on chapters 6 and 7. Watch it prior to your discussion of chapter 6.

Link to video 1: crossrivermedia.com/unshakable1
Link to video 2: crossrivermedia.com/unshakable2
Link to video 3: crossrivermedia.com/unshakable3

CHAPTER 1

WHO IS GOD?

So don't be afraid, little flock. For it gives your Father great happiness to give you the Kingdom. Luke 12:32 NLT

Lesson 1
What Is the Kingdom?

How can we live a life of unshakable faith in God's Kingdom without first understanding what the Kingdom of God is?

As I've read verses like Matthew 6:33, "seek first the kingdom of God," and Luke 17:21, "For indeed, the kingdom of God is within you," I wondered exactly what *was* God's Kingdom. If I didn't know what His Kingdom was, how could I seek it and how could I know for sure if His Kingdom was within me?

And then there are verses like 2 Peter 1:3, "As His divine power has given to us all things that pertain to life and godliness, through the knowledge of Him who called us by glory and virtue." This verse more than any other piqued my desire and spurred my search to understand God's Kingdom. Because for me, life was a constant struggle to survive. Even though I believed in God and was a born-again Christian, I lacked joy. I felt my life did not reflect the truth of any of these verses.

Merriam-Webster's Collegiate Dictionary defines kingdom as "a politically organized community or major territorial unit having a monarchical form of government headed by a king or queen."

As an American living under the rule of a republic—by the people and for the people—kingdom rule was hard for me to grasp. It would seem that during my growing years I unconsciously took in the concept of autonomy, the state of being self-governed. I don't like the idea of being ruled by anyone. It connotes dictatorship, living under a ruler who does what's best for him no matter the cost to his citizens. History is replete with kings who lived in luxury beyond our comprehension while his citizens toiled endlessly to support the king's lifestyle, but they themselves lived in hovels with barely enough to feed their family. Of such are revolutions made.

Having lived four years in Germany and visiting many places and other countries, I saw firsthand the opulence of kings' castles. The Palace of Versailles in France was particularly eye-opening. The total acreage is 2,014 acres, which includes 230 acres of gardens.[1] By way of comparison, a football field is 1.1 acre. The palace itself contains 679,783 square feet of floorspace,[2] roughly fourteen football fields. The Hall of Mirrors, the most famous room of the palace is just short of eighty yards in length and contains 357 mirrors.[3] And I haven't even mentioned all the gold! No wonder the French revolted.

Heaven has an opulence all its own, and I'm so glad God doesn't make me work to furnish it!

Merriam-Webster's also offers this definition: "the realm in which God's will is fulfilled." That definition brings to mind Matthew 6:10, "Your kingdom come, Your will be done," and

1. Wikipedia

2. Wikipedia

3. http://en.chateauversailles.fr/discover/estate/palace/hall-mirrors

Jeremiah 29:11, "For I know the thoughts that I think toward you, says the LORD, thoughts of peace and not of evil, to give you a future and a hope." That definition I can embrace.

I am of the Baby Boomer Generation, raised by parents who lived through the Great Depression and who both served in the US Marine Corps during World War II. I grew up under the strict disciplinary hand of my father. My siblings and I received spankings when we disobeyed or behaved wrongly. My childhood was "do as you're told or else."

I feared my father, and the Bible told me to fear the LORD God. Consequently, I saw God in the same light as I saw my father—someone who was very strict and to be afraid of.

When I surrendered my life to God and accepted Jesus as Lord and Savior, it was not the experience I had often heard from others—coming joyfully to the altar to find forgiveness for sins.

I attended the Methodist church as a child and learned the usual Bible stories taught in Sunday school—Tower of Babel, Noah's Ark, Mary and Joseph going to Bethlehem, baby Jesus. I believed in God and believed Jesus died to save me, but God was not the ruler of my life. Up to that point He was someone who punished me when I did wrong. I saw all the bad things that happened in my life as coming from Him—His punishment for misbehaving. At the age of twenty-four the circumstances in my life had become unbearable. My Marine husband was at sea, serving aboard a Navy ship, and had been for months. My three-year-old was yelling from the bathroom for something he needed. I felt like I was in a wrestling match, and as I stood in the middle of the kitchen, I cried out, "Okay, God. I give up. I'll accept you as the Lord of my life."

But that is far from who God is and what His Kingdom is. God spent many years teaching me who He really is. To be honest, it took decades for me to grasp how much God loves me. I wish it hadn't taken me so long to learn. Over the years

I've also come to realize that the church as a whole, as the body of Christ, has fallen short in discipling those who accept Jesus as Lord, those who are born again. That is what has spurred the writing of this Bible study.

As you progress through this study, I pray you will discover God, His mercy, and His grace, and marvel at what living in His Kingdom truly means.

Lesson 2
Grasping the Depth of God's Love

For various reasons many people struggle with feeling unworthy, unlovable, or not valuable enough to be part of the Kingdom. I was one of those people.

How can we live fully in the Kingdom if we aren't convinced we belong there?

At this very moment, as God looks at you, how do you think He sees you and thinks about you?

It is natural to view God as we view our earthly fathers. Was your father loving and accepting? Perhaps he was emotionally or physically absent. Was he abusive?

My father was of the Builder Generation (aka the Silent Generation, those born between 1924 and 1945). He was very strict and a spanking came swiftly if I disobeyed or did something wrong. My difficulty was I often didn't understand what I did wrong to warrant his anger and punishment. I grew up afraid of him and did everything I knew to do to earn his love. I carried that fear and performance into my relationship with God.

Stop and think about the character of your earthly father and the relationship you have/had with him. How has it affected your relationship with God?

Have you grown up believing you must perform to earn God's love?

Read Matthew 7:9–11 and Galatians 4:5–7. What do these verses say to you?

Do you struggle to grasp that God really loves you, faults and all? Why or why not?

Read John 3:16 (perhaps you already know it by memory) and 1 John 4:9.

Think about the depth of commitment involved in dying in someone else's place and write your thoughts here.

That's what Jesus did for us. He did it because the Father asked Him to. And the Father asked because He knew we were incapable of living a perfect life. God's holiness demands holiness; sin cannot reside in His presence.

How is God's love shown in Romans 5:6–8?

Why do you think God sent His Son to die for us?

Read Romans 8:35–39.

Is there anything that might happen to you or that you might do that would make God stop loving you? Why or why not?

After studying the above verses, has your perception of God's love changed? If so, how?

Read the following verses and write a brief statement about what each verse says.

Psalms 139:1–18

Isaiah 43:1

Jeremiah 31:3

Zephaniah 3:17

Luke 12:7

Ephesians 2:10 (I especially like the NLT, which states we are His masterpiece.)

1 John 3:1

How do you feel knowing this is how God sees you?

God loves you! So much so He sent Jesus to die in your place to pay the price for your sins (John 3:16) so you could be reconciled to God and live eternally in heaven.

Jesus died for you! Stop and think about all that means. What does it say to you?

If you are a parent, would you die in your child's place if it meant your child could live?

Our value lies in who God says we are, not what people say. The Bible also says:

You are the apple of his eye. (Zechariah 2:8)

He loves you with an unfailing love. (Psalm 117:2)

The LORD is your security. (Proverbs 3:26)

Resting securely in God's love is part and parcel of living strong in God's Kingdom.

Lesson 3
Who Is God?

How can we live in the fullness of all God has for us if we don't understand who God is?

If you asked 100 people, I expect you'd get 100 different answers. But if I want to get to know someone, I don't ask other people about that person. Instead, I get acquainted directly.

In the space provided below, write down who you think God is. Do you see Him as kind and benevolent, or is He waiting to punish you the very moment you make a mistake? Be honest in your answer so you can learn and grow in your knowledge of Him.

As Christians we live under God's rule, His Kingdom, so it's important to have more than a passing acquaintance of Him. If we don't spend time getting to know Him, we can trivialize Him. He becomes some *thing* out there in the ether or a magic genie whom we call upon to grant us our every wish. But He is the Creator of the heavens and the earth (see Genesis 1) and He keeps it all working (Colossians 1:17)!

The best way to get to know God is to spend time reading His Word, the Bible. So let's dive in and learn who God says He is.

In your Bible, turn to Exodus 3:6. In this passage, God is speaking to Moses from the burning bush. What does He tell Moses about who He is?

Moses knew the Israelites were an obstinate people, so he wanted more specificity. He asks God His name. What was God's answer in verse 14?

From *Strong's Concordance* (a book that shows the original language of the Bible and each word's meaning), the Hebrew word *hayah*, translated here as I AM, means "to be, exist."

Now let's look at Exodus 34:5. What does God proclaim His name to be?

In this verse, God gives His proper name, which the Hebrews wrote as *YHWH*, meaning Self-Existent or Eternal. (In the early stages of the Hebrew language there were no vowels.)

The point I want to make here is that God wasn't saying quite the same thing each time. To the Israelites, God's word choices revealed different aspects of Himself. In translation to English we often lose that information. For that very reason, throughout this chapter we're going to look at the original language to better grasp the depth of who God says He is.

When you see the word LORD, in small capital letters, understand He is using his proper name (like my proper name is Debra), and He is speaking to His self-existence. It is sometimes rendered as Jehovah. The Israelites considered God's proper name too holy to speak, and they dared not speak it.

When we see *Lord* (upper and lower case), it is the word the Israelites used as a proper name when addressing God, *adonay*, meaning master.

Turn to Genesis 22:14. What does this verse reveal to us about God?

Depending on the translation you are using, you'll see *The Lord Will Provide* or *Jehovahjireh*, in Hebrew, *YHWH-jireh*. God is telling us through this name that He provides for all our needs.

Now turn to Psalm 11:7 and Jeremiah 23:6. How is God described here?

In Jeremiah 23:6, the Hebrew is *The LORD our righteousness, YHWH-tsidqenu (Jehovah Tsidqenu)*. God is making reference to Christ. Christ is God incarnate. He is the righteous judge of everyone, believer and non-believer. As the righteous judge, God accepts Christ's sacrifice on the cross as payment for our sins. When we accept Jesus as our Savior we put on, or are clothed with, Christ's righteousness. From that point on, when God looks at us, He sees Christ's righteousness.

Now let's take a look Judges 6:24. What did Gideon name the altar he built?

We need not worry or be afraid because *YHWH-shalom, the LORD is peace (Jehovah-Shalom)*, gives us peace for all our circumstances.

Turn to Ezekiel 48:35. This verse refers to Jerusalem, the City of God. What do we learn about God through what the city is named?

In the Hebrew, *YHWH-shammah (Jehovah Shammah)* means "the LORD is there." He is always with us.

Read Exodus 15:26 and write down His name.

In the Hebrew, He is *YHWH-rapha*, *(Jehovah Rapha)*, *the* LORD *our healer.* He heals us spiritually, physically, mentally, and emotionally.

Let's take a look at one last Scripture, Psalm 23:1. How is God described?

In the Hebrew, *YHWH-rohi*, *the* LORD *is our Shepherd.* He cares for us and provides all we need.

In each of these names, God reveals an aspect of Himself. This is only a very small portion of who He is. The depth of God is beyond what we can comprehend.

Up to this point in your walk with God, how have you known Him?

Describe one or two situations in your life where God has demonstrated Himself to you in one of the above manners.

Do you need peace? God is our Jehovah-Shalom. Is it healing you need? He is our Jehovah-Rapha. Provision for daily needs? He is our provider, Jehovah-Jireh. All we need, we can find in God.

In the next section, we'll discover God's attributes.

Lesson 4
Attributes of God

In this lesson we'll look at God's attributes, because if we do not have a full understanding of who and what He is, we are too easily swayed by Satan's deceptions. In looking at the names of God, we also saw how those names described some of His attributes. An attribute is a "quality, character, or characteristic ascribed to someone or something."[4]

As a child at school I learned about the gods of Greek and Roman mythology. Zeus, Apollo, Hera, Aphrodite, Neptune, and others. My Sunday school teacher taught me about the false gods of the nations that surrounded Israel and whom many Israelites eventually began to worship.

These so-called gods were supposedly immortal, but they most certainly were not perfect. The Roman and Greek gods got angry often and were rarely pleased with what mankind attempted to do for them. These gods made good fodder for storytelling, but that's all. Indeed, my mind struggles to comprehend why anyone would worship such fickle, imperfect gods.

The false gods named in the Bible were demanding and angry all the time. None contributed to the life and well-being of their worshipers. They couldn't contribute, because these gods were non-existent (see Psalm 115:4–7). They were the creations of man's imagination.

At this point in your walk with God, what attributes of God do you know? List them below.

---

4. *Merriam-Webster Collegiate Dictionary*, http://unabridged.merriam-webster.com/collegiate/attribute

Now, let's examine His attributes.

Read Psalm 103:19. This verse says God rules over all/everything. What does that mean to you?

Now read 2 Chronicles 20:6 and Jeremiah 32:17. What character trait do these verses express?

Read the following and note what they tell you about God.

Psalm 147:5

Isaiah 40:12–14

Job 21:22

Does He know every thought you'll think today and every day forward (and all your yesterdays, too)?

Does He know the very place you'll be one year from now? Five years? Ten years?

Does He know the very day, hour, minute, and second of your death?

The answer to each of these questions is a resounding yes! God is omniscient. He knows everything—past, present, future. How does that make you feel?

Read the following verses: Romans 1:20, Job 37:23, and Nehemiah 9:6. What do they tell you about God?

No creature—natural or supernatural—can overpower God. When I stopped to consider this, I realized I believed Satan was just as powerful as God. How I ever came to believe that, I don't know, but when I realized it, I immediately replaced that lie with the truth: nothing and no one is more powerful than God.

How does knowing that God is sovereign over all, omniscient, and all-powerful impact your faith in Him?

Note what attribute you find in the following verses.

Jeremiah 23:23–24

Psalm 139:7–10

Proverbs 15:3

It's hard to comprehend that God is with you this very moment as you read this Bible study and also with that two-year-old orphan in India and that soul in the Middle East who will be martyred today.

As I learned and meditated on these attributes, they instilled an awe of God within me. However, before I knew the full extent of God's character, Satan used these same attributes to cause fear within me—that proverbial bolt of lightning if I did something wrong.

Lesson 5
God's Attributes, cont'd

Now let's look at some aspects of God we rarely consider—or perhaps don't even know—but are as important as the ones from yesterday's lesson.

What do the following verses tell you about God?

Exodus 3:14

Isaiah 44:6

Revelation 1:8

Perhaps you've never thought about it, but nothing and no one created or gave birth to God. He always was and always will be. He is Self-Existent.

Now read these verses and list the attributes described.

Isaiah 40:28

John 5:26 (The NLT states it this way: "The Father has life in himself, and he has granted that same life-giving power to his Son.")

John 15:5

God does not grow weary or hungry or lonely. He needs nothing to sustain His existence. He is Self-Sufficient. He is perfect and complete within Himself.

Quite often we learn about several attributes in one verse. Such is the case with Isaiah 40:28, which speaks to God's Self-Existence, Self-Sufficiency, and His omniscience.

Read Psalm 145:8–9. What do these say about God?

Next let's look at God's holiness.
In your own words write down what it means to be holy.

According to the *Merriam-Webster Collegiate Dictionary*, holy means "exalted or worthy of complete devotion as one perfect in goodness and righteousness."
Read Leviticus 11:44.
In this verse, God is telling the people to consecrate themselves. To consecrate is "to make or declare sacred."[5] In the original language of this verse *consecrate* means to be clean, pure.
Read Isaiah 6:1–5.
Beholding the holiness of God in His throne room, what does Isaiah discover about himself?

The same Hebrew word for *holy* used in Leviticus 11:44 is used in this passage from Isaiah and means sacred. I especially like the way *Gesenius' Hebrew-Chaldee Lexicon* describes *holy*: "pure, clean, free from defilement of crimes, idolatry, and other unclean and profane things."
As Isaiah beheld the holiness (infinite purity) of God, he discovered the depth of his own impure condition.
Lest we think holiness was only for the Old Testament, let's read 1 Peter 1:15–16. What does it say about us?

---

5. *Merriam-Webster's Collegiate Dictionary* online

When we come to Christ, we are all in the same state of impurity as Isaiah was. When we accept Christ as Lord and Savior, He makes us clean and clothes us with His purity.

Read Malachi 3:6 and Psalm 102:25–27, then write down what this tells you about God.

This attribute is known as immutability; God does not change. When I first learned this, it made a huge impact on me. At that point in my life, I knew too many people who acted one way about an issue one day and acted the opposite way the next day. I was projecting that same characteristic on God. Knowing He never changes brought a lot of peace to my spirit.

To fully grasp that God cannot change allows us to kick our doubts and distrust to the curb and trust Him without reserve.

Have you ever thought about the above attributes? Write down two or three sentences about how this knowledge impacts your faith and trust in God.

Next, let's turn to some well-known, but often misunderstood attributes.

Lesson 6
God's Grace and Mercy

What attributes of God do you think are at work when we accept Christ's death as payment for our sins?

What do you learn about God's grace in Ephesians 2:8 and Hebrews 4:16?

What do you learn about God's mercy in Titus 3:5 and Psalm 103:17 (your translation may read *love* or *lovingkindness*)?

What does faithfulness mean to you?

Let's look at *faithful* and *faithfulness* in the original language. Read Hebrews 10:23 (one of my favorite verses).

The word *faithful* as used here means trustworthy. "For God can be trusted to keep his promise" (Hebrews 10:23b NLT).

In earthly relationships trust is earned. We are taking a step of faith when we trust God for our salvation. After that, we continue to take steps of faith, and our trust in God grows as He brings answers to our prayers or provides blessings in unexpected ways.

34   DEBRA L. BUTTERFIELD

No relationship can survive without trust. If you struggle trusting God and knowing He is faithful, read the following verses. Jot down what they speak to you.

Numbers 23:19

Deuteronomy 7:9

Psalm 36:5

Psalm 119:89, 90a

Matthew 24:35

1 Thessalonians 5:24

2 Timothy 2:13

Consider all you've learned in this section on who God is. How has what you've learned changed your perception of God?

Do you have a favorite attribute, one that speaks to your heart more than any other at this moment in your life? List it here and write a brief two or three sentences as to why.

Without God's grace, mercy, and love, it would be all too easy to view Him as an angry and demanding judge. God is love, but He doesn't ignore grace, mercy, faithfulness, or any of His other attributes as He extends His love to us.

There is no doubt about it. Grasping these attributes of God is hard for our finite brains. But for God to be any less in any one of these areas would make Him less than perfect, fallible, and thus, unworthy of the rank of God, and unworthy of our worship.

Trusting God is a choice. But understanding all these attributes will give you a firm foundation of who God really is, why He is worthy of our worship, and why we can fully trust Him with our lives and rest (not worry) in His promises.

Here is what God says about Himself:

"I publicly proclaim bold promises.

I do not whisper obscurities in some dark corner.

I would not have told the people of Israel to seek me

if I could not be found.

I, the LORD, speak only what is true

and declare only what is right." (Isaiah 45:19 NLT)

Wow! God is amazing.

As we grow in understanding the names and attributes of God, it sets the stage for us to learn more about living in the Kingdom.

"Oh, how great are God's riches and wisdom and knowledge! How impossible it is for us to understand his decisions and his ways! For who can know the LORD's thoughts? Who knows enough to give him advice? And who has given him so much that he needs to pay it back? For everything comes from him and exists by his power and is intended for his glory. All glory to him forever! Amen." Romans 11:33–36 NLT

(For a more in-depth understanding of God's attributes, read *The Knowledge of the Holy* by A.W. Tozer)

Chapter 2

Our Kingdom Identity

Lesson 1
Covenant of the Law

*"And you will know the truth and the truth
will make you free." (John 8:32)*

In February 1974, I took the US Armed Forces Oath of Enlistment. At that moment, I was enlisted into the US Marine Corps even though I was still a senior in high school. I was scheduled to leave for boot camp in July. Between February and July there was no changing my mind. I was already a part of the USMC.

By way of analogy, when we accept Jesus as Savior, much the same thing happens, only infinitely better! We become citizens of heaven and all the blessings of heaven are now available and accessible to us.

List here the benefits you believe the kingdom of heaven has for you.

Satan thrills in deceiving us about God and His Kingdom, so let's spend some time here discussing two very important items: the covenant of the law and the covenant of grace.

In today's world of contracts, grasping the depth of covenant can be confusing, maybe even difficult. *Covenant* and *contract* are not synonymous; you cannot switch equally one for the other.

Merriam-Webster Dictionary defines the act of covenant as "to promise by a covenant : pledge." Like a contract, a covenant is sealed in some manner: an oath, by blood, a signature, a handshake. A contract can be broken and is broken when one of the parties doesn't do what was agreed to.

A covenant is binding; it *cannot* be broken. If one party cannot meet the obligations of the covenant, the other party provides what is lacking.

I'm sure that's all clear as a cloudy sky, so let's look first at the covenant of the law.

The covenant of the law—the Ten Commandments and all the ritual laws, over 600 of them—was between God and the Jewish people. Satan attempts to deceive us into believing this covenant was between God and all mankind. *It was only for the Jew.* Its purpose was to show the Jews their sin, but it never had the power to transform them. Gentiles were never under or bound by the covenant of the law! Unless you were born of Jewish parents, you are a Gentile.

Turn to Deuteronomy 28:1. As you read, note specifically the verbiage "if you" (*if thou* in KJV), "God will."

What did God want the Israelites to do?

If the Israelites obeyed God's commands, what did God promise to do? Read verses 2–13.

Verses 3 through 13 outline all the blessings God would bring if the Israelites obeyed all His commands.

Verses 15 through 68 outline all that would happen if they didn't obey. Eleven verses of blessings, fifty-four verses of curses.

Have you ever found yourself performing in order to get God to do something?

Let me put that question another way. Have you ever said to God during prayer, "I read your Word every day," or "I go to church every week," or "I'm doing my best not to sin…why aren't You answering my prayers?"

If you answered yes to any of those (or anything similar), you are caught in performance. Don't berate yourself if you are. I was there myself for way too many years.

Our society focuses on performance. Oftentimes even our parents' love is conditional on our performance. Is it any wonder that we slip into performance mode with God?

But He has a better plan!

Lesson 2
Covenant of Grace

Let's do a quick review of the last lesson on the covenant of the law. It was between God and the Jewish people, and it was based on performance. Its purpose was to show the Jews their sin, but never had the power to transform them. Remember also, that a covenant is binding and that if one party can't meet its obligations, the other party makes up for the lack. The Jews were constantly unfaithful to the law.

Now let's look at the covenant of grace.

The covenant of grace is between God and Jesus. Read Matthew 5:17–18. According to these, what did Jesus come to do?

Jesus led a sinless life. He was faithful to and met every condition of the Law!

Read Exodus 12:1–11. What did the Israelites have to do to be protected from the angel of death?

Now read John 1:29 and 1 Corinthians 5:7. What do these say about Jesus in relation to the slain lamb of Exodus 12?

Turn to Hebrews 8:6–7, 13. What is the first covenant referred to in verse 7?

Jesus fulfilled the law, but His ultimate act of dying on the cross and shedding His blood obtained for us the "better covenant" spoken of in verse 6.

Read John 3:16–17.

We enter into the covenant of grace when we believe in Jesus and His sacrifice for us. What God does for us has nothing to do with our behavior or how we perform, whether we deserve something or not. God does what He does because of His covenant with Jesus.

Performance is the currency of the law, but faith is the currency of grace. See Ephesians 2:8 and Hebrews 11:6.

A contrast of law and grace from Creflo Dollar Ministries.

Covenant of Law	Covenant of Grace
Is between God & Jewish people	Is between God and Jesus
Kills	Gives life
Is about man's lack of faithfulness	Is about Jesus' faithfulness
Shines light on sin	Shines light on Jesus' perfection
Designed to bring out man's sin	Designed to make men holy
Brings condemnation	Brings justification
Causes sin consciousness	Causes righteousness consciousness
Covers sin with blood of animal	Takes away sin by Jesus' blood

Lesson 3
Our Old Nature, Our New Nature

To live strong in God's Kingdom it's important we fully understand what happened to us when we accepted Christ as our Savior. It can be difficult to grasp because it's a change we cannot see with our physical eyes.

Read Romans 6:6. The "old man" refers to our human nature, not our physical body.

Read the following verses and list what they state is the nature of the new man.

Ephesians 4:24

Romans 6:17–18

2 Corinthians 5:17

1 John 3:9

Read the following verses and write a brief statement about what each says.

Ephesians 2:3–7

1 Corinthians 2:12

Ephesians 1:18–20

Ephesians 2:19

Philippians 3:20

But there's more.

Read Galatians 4:5–7 and Ephesians 1:5. What do these verses have to say about who we are?

Since God is King of kings and Lord of lords, as His children, what does that make us?

As a child of the King, you are either a princess or prince. You may not feel like a princess (or prince), but that's what you are—a child of the King! How does thinking of yourself as royalty make you feel?

Lesson 4
How Does this Identity in Christ Help Me?

It's wonderful to know our identity in Christ. Knowing how much God truly loves us gives us strength every day, not just during our battles. But there is so much more that comes with being in Christ. (If needed, review the lesson "How God Sees Us" from chapter 1.)

Read the following and write a brief statement about each.

John 15:5

Acts 17:28

Luke 10:19

2 Peter 1:3

Stop and think about what those verses are telling you. Did anything in particular jump out at you? If so, write it down.

Write down anything from these verses that challenge how you've been living your life.

It is God's grace and the power of the Holy Spirit (more on this later) that enable us to do all we do. Apart from Him we can do nothing (Acts 17:28). In Christ, we have both the ability (power) and right (authority) to rule over the enemy. As His children, we have access to God's power and resources.

Satan has no power or authority over us, but he tries to deceive us into believing he does.

Read 2 Corinthians 10:3–5.

What does verse 4 say about our weapons?

What does verse 5 tells us we are to do?

Let's take a closer look at 2 Peter 1:2–4. According to verse 3, what has God given us?

According to verse 4?

Now let's look at a couple more verses for emphasis.

Romans 8:32

Ephesians 3:20

Philippians 4:19

God not only provides for our every spiritual need, but also our physical/natural needs. After all, what kind of Father would He be if He only provided for part of our needs?

If you got out of bed every day reminding yourself that God provides for all your needs, how would that impact you and your day?

Satan doesn't want us to know God or to grasp all He has given us. But we must learn the truths of the Bible in order to recognize and refute deception.

We'll take a much deeper look into our weapons of warfare and spiritual armor in later chapters. For now, learning these basic truths about your identity and that God has provided all you need to live a godly life is the beginning of a strong foundation in Christ and living in His Kingdom.

Lesson 5
What Does God Desire for Us?

M any people believe God is sitting up in heaven waiting for us to do something wrong so He can punish us. If that were the true character of God, who would want to worship Him?

Of course, Satan wants us to believe that, but let's examine that by looking at God's character of justice.

What do the following verses say about God and judgment?

Ecclesiastes 3:17

Hebrews 10:30

Isaiah 30:18

To believe God is counting the minutes until He can punish you is to totally misunderstand the character of God—He is a God of justice.

Do loving parents wait with anticipation for moments when they can punish their children? Of course not! They discipline their children, when necessary, to teach them right from wrong, and they establish rules to protect them. God does likewise.

Unfortunately many of us relate justice only to the meting out of punishment. But justice is making a determination of action based on the rules of law.

Read 1 John 4:7–8. What do these verses express to you?

What does 1 John 4:18 say about God?

The Amplified Bible gives greater insight into this verse.

"There is no fear in love [dread does not exist]. But perfect (complete, full-grown) love drives out fear, because fear involves [the expectation of divine] punishment, so the one who is afraid [of God's judgment] is not perfected in love [has not grown into a sufficient understanding of God's love]."

Read the following verses and write down what they say about God's desire for our lives.

John 10:10

Romans 8:28

Jeremiah 29:11

Isaiah 58:11

One morning during my quiet time with God I pondered why it is so difficult for Christians (myself included) to believe all the promises God has made us. We believe Christ died for us. One man died to pay the price for our sins—all believers and their sins, past, present, and future! We believe *that*, yet why is it so hard to believe we are healed or that He has provided for all our needs or any of the other hundreds of promises He has made us?

If God was not faithful to His promises, what message would that send to His Son who died to redeem us and secure those promises for us?

What do each of the following verses have to say about God's faithfulness to His promises?

Numbers 23:19

1 Kings 8:56

Psalm 138:2

Hebrews 6:13

Hebrews 10:23

2 Peter 3:9

God is faithful. Open your heart to believe and receive all that He promises!

Lesson 6
What Does God Want from Us?

God is a God of abundance and He freely gives. He gives out of His love, grace, and mercy. We do not work for our salvation, and we do not work to earn His blessings. *Deserve* never enters the picture. God blesses us out of His love for us. He wants us to be filled with joy, and our joy brings glory to Jesus.

Do you think we are a part of the Kingdom merely to enjoy its pleasures? Explain your answer.

Read John 6:29. What does God want us to do?

Turn to Matthew 5:13–16. What do these verses say we are?

What has Christ commanded us to do?

Read Ephesians 6:20. How does Paul describe himself?

Look up the word *ambassador* in the dictionary and write a brief description here.

Do you see yourself as an ambassador for Christ? Why or why not?

Read 1 Peter 2:9. What does God call us in this verse?

What does He say He wants us to do?

Read Romans 8:29 and Romans 12:2.

What does it mean to you to "be conformed to the image of his Son"? (Your Bible might say "become like.")

According to *Strong's Concordance*, *conformed* in the original language means "to fashion alike."

I have two older brothers. As they have aged, they have physically looked more and more like our father. When family and friends who knew our father see my brothers, they know immediately who their father was because they look so much like him.

As His chosen people, do you think God wants us to look like Christ? Why or why not?

How does the maxim "Actions speak louder than words" affect being conformed to the image of Christ?

God desires that when strangers look at us, they see the family resemblance to His Son Jesus. Not that we physically look like Him, but that the peace and love of Jesus are evident in all our actions and words.

As it says in Jeremiah 29:11, God has a plan for each of us. Read Romans 12:4–21. Do you see yourself in these verses? Explain your answer.

Have you begun to sense God's plan for your life? If not, ask Him. We each fit into the Body of Christ, and our skills and talents often point the way to how and where we fit into His plan.

Read Ephesians 4:11–16, 1 Peter 4:10–11, and 1 Corinthians 12:4–11.

We have each been given a special gift. We operate in our gift in order to equip God's people and build up the church.

As we function within our place in the Body, it helps other parts grow so that the "whole body is healthy and growing and full of love" (Ephesians 4:16 NLT).

Spend some time today and ask God what His plan/vision is for your life and where you fit into the Body. Write your thoughts here or in your journal.

Whenever you feel you don't measure up, remind yourself that God sees you as righteous. He sees you that way because of your acceptance of Christ's sacrifice for your life. God loves you and nothing will change that! He has a plan for your life and that plan is for good, not evil.

"Can anything ever separate us from Christ's love? Does it mean he no longer loves us if we have trouble or calamity, or are persecuted, or hungry, or destitute, or in danger, or threatened with death?...And I am convinced that nothing can ever separate us from God's love. Neither death nor life, neither angels nor demons, neither our fears for today nor our worries about tomorrow—not even the powers of hell can separate us from God's love. No power in the sky above or in the earth below—indeed, nothing in all creation will ever be able to separate us from the love of God that is revealed in Christ Jesus our Lord" (Romans 8:35, 37–39 NLT).

CHAPTER 3

WHO ELSE IS A MAJOR PLAYER?

Lesson 1
Who is Jesus?

*The reason the Son of God was made manifest (visible)
was to undo (destroy, loosen, and dissolve) the works
the devil [has done]. (1 John 3:8 AMPCE)*

Most Christians will readily respond that Jesus is the Son of
God and that He died to pay the price for our sins. He is so
much more!

When you think of Jesus, what comes to mind?

Read the following and list what they say about who Jesus is.

Matthew 1:23

John 1:1–3

John 1:14

John 10:11

John 14:6

Colossians 1:15

Colossians 1:18

Colossians 2:9

In John 10:11, Jesus said He is the good Shepherd. So let's turn to Psalm 23, one of the most well-known and among the most popular of all the psalms. List the attributes shown here and all the things the Shepherd does for us, His sheep.

Vs. 1

Vs. 2

Vs. 3

Vs. 4

Vs. 5

Vs. 6

Read the following verses and list what Jesus did for us.

Matthew 20:28

John 3:16

Acts 4:12

Romans 5:8

2 Corinthians 5:21

Colossians 1:13

Whole books can be written on who Jesus is and what He does for us. He is God with us, and He paid the price for our sins first by fulfilling the Law and then by dying on the cross in our place. Hallelujah! We don't have to earn our way to heaven. Christ did that for us!

For a fuller list of all Christ has done for us, turn to the appendix "Who I Am in Christ."

Lesson 2
Who is the Holy Spirit?

If there is one person of the Trinity (the triune being of God the Father, Jesus the Son, and the Holy Spirit) who is rarely spoken about, it is Holy Spirit. But we ignore Holy Spirit at our peril. He is an intimate part of our lives here on Earth.

List below what you know about who Holy Spirit is and what He does.

Read the following verses and list what each says concerning the Holy Spirit.

John 7:37–39

John 14:16–18

Ephesians 1:13–14

Galatians 4:6

What is Holy Spirit's function? Read the following verses.

Nehemiah 9:20

John 14:26

John 16:7–13

Acts 1:8

Acts 2:1–5

Romans 8:26–27

Now let's turn to Galatians 5:16–25.

Verse 18 states we are led (*directed* in NLT) by the Spirit. What is our responsibility in that?

The original Greek word translated *walk* in this verse is *sto-cichéō*, and it means "to march in (military) rank (keep step)."

As a Marine, I can understand that! When a military platoon walks in rank, everyone is making the *same* step, with the *same* foot, at the *same* moment. A platoon leader (who walks beside the platoon) is calling out commands—forward march, column right, to the rear, halt—and the platoon executes those commands, moving as one body, not as forty individuals.

So if we are living our lives by the leading of the Spirit, what do you think our lives will look like?

In following Holy Spirit, He will not prompt you to do anything that contradicts God's Word. There are spirits that are not of God, and Satan can plant thoughts in our mind. So when you wonder about the thoughts in your mind telling you to do this or that, check it against God's Word. Does it speak truth?

Lesson 3
Who is the Real Enemy?

Years ago, when it came to light that my husband was sexually abusing my daughter, one of the first things I had to realize was that my husband was not my enemy. The lawyers and social workers weren't my enemies. The multitude of bad events wasn't my enemy. The devil was. How did I know that? Because Ephesians 6:12 told me: "For we do not wrestle against flesh and blood, but against principalities, against powers, against the rulers of the darkness of this age, against spiritual *hosts* of wickedness in the heavenly *places*." (NKJV)

There are ministers who preach that Hell and Satan do not exist. But the Bible is quite adamant that they do. In this lesson, we're going to take a look at who Satan is. It is important to know who he is and how he works so we can recognize when he (and his cohorts) shows up in our lives.

What does the Bible have to say about Satan? Read Ezekiel 28:11–19 and list his characteristics here.

While verse 11 refers to the king of Tyre, we know that no earthly king was in the Garden of Eden or could be an "anointed cherub who covers." Bible scholars believe these verses to be a comparison of the king of Tyre and Satan.

Satan was an angel created by God, the seal of perfection and covered with precious stones. But then pride was found in his heart, and he was cast out of heaven.

What are some of his names?

Job 1:6

Isaiah 14:12

Matthew 4:1

Matthew 13:19

John 8:44

John 14:30

Ephesians 2:1–3

Revelation 12:10

In Job 1:6 we learn Satan came before God to make accusations against Job. We find in *Strong's Concordance* the original Hebrew word used for Satan in this verse is *satan*, meaning *adversary*. (I've always wondered how he got that name.)

Do you think Satan does the same thing concerning us or was that limited only to Job? Why or why not?

Now read Luke 22:31. Does that change your answer above? Why or why not?

Now read Luke 22:32 and then 1 John 2:1–2. In relation to Satan accusing and attacking us, what does Jesus do for us?

Take heart, Jesus has already defeated Satan. We'll learn more about that in a later lesson.

Lesson 4
What are Satan's Powers?

Often, without realizing, we believe something is true that actually is a lie. Many of those truths are accepted while we are children and not knowledgeable in the Bible or mature enough to know the difference.

During my quiet time one day, God revealed to me that I had come to believe Satan was as powerful as God. Wow! That is as far from the truth as the east is from the west.

In the previous lesson we learned God created Satan. Satan is not self-existent, not all-powerful, cannot be in more than one place at a time, and cannot read my thoughts—no verse in the Bible tells us angels are omniscient. Only God is omniscient.

As a created being, Satan's existence is dependent on God. If God chose to, He could destroy Satan at any time.

Read the following verses and take note of some of the things Satan does.

Job 2:7

Matthew 4:1

Matthew 4:6–7

Acts 10:38

2 Corinthians 4:4

2 Corinthians 11:14

Read John 10:10 and 1 Peter 5:8. What does Satan want to do to us?

Satan once held the power of death. Who destroyed that power? Read Hebrews 2:14.

Who now holds the keys to death and hell? Read Revelation 1:17–18.

Our victory over death is accomplished when we believe Christ died to redeem us from death and accept Him as Savior (John 3:16, 12:46, and Acts 26:18).

Now let's examine how Satan works. Read Genesis 3:1–13.

In verse 1, Satan (the serpent) says, "Indeed, has God said, 'You shall not eat from any tree of the garden'?" Was this really what God said? Read Genesis 2:16–17 to find the answer.

When God asked Eve what had happened in the Garden, what was her response? (See verse 13.)

Read Revelation 12:9. What does this verse say Satan does?

One of Satan's most powerful weapons against us is deceit. And he often uses God's Word to deceive us. He knows the Bible as well as, if not better than, we do. That's why it is so vital we read the Bible and know what it says, what God's promises are, and what our identity as children of God is.

If we don't know the truth, we can't recognize a lie!

Think about your life up to this point. Is there an area (or two or three) where Satan has deceived you? List it here.

Lesson 5
Replace Lies with the Truth

The second half of John 17:17 tells us "Your word is truth." John 8:32 says, "And you will know the truth, and the truth will set you free."

To know truth, we need to read the Bible. There we find God's truths to refute any lies we might have already believed or that are inundating us now. In all things, the Bible is our reference point for truth!

Today, spend your study time asking God to reveal any lies you have embraced as truth. Write them here or in your journal. I'll prompt you with some questions to help you get started.

- Are there areas where you struggle with the same problem(s) over and over again? This is a pretty good indication you've believed a lie. As you think about that problem, ask God to reveal any lies you believe as truth.

- Do you believe you are loved unconditionally by God? If not, why? Ask what the root of that belief is. Is there an event(s) in your life that has made you believe God doesn't love you?

- Do you believe God wants you to be successful (however you might define that for yourself)?

- Do you believe God wants you to be healthy?

Let Holy Spirit lead you. Sit quietly as you ask your questions and expect an answer. Some situations might take longer to receive an answer. Persevere and continue to ask.

"For we do not wrestle against flesh and blood, but against principalities, against powers, against the rulers of the darkness of this age, against spiritual hosts *of wickedness in the heavenly* places" *(Ephesians 6:12 NKJV).*

PART TWO:

FUNCTIONING
IN THE KINGDOM

*For every child of God defeats this evil world, and we
achieve this victory through our faith. (1 John 5:4 NLT)*

Here is where our boots hit the ground. We've graduated from basic training and now we're advancing to tech school. Okay, think of it this way: It's like graduating from high school and heading off to college.

In part 2, we're going to dive into what it looks like to live out our lives 100% in the Kingdom of God.

I truly believe that until the day the Lord takes me home, I'll be learning and growing in faith. This is a journey! I'm still learning. You're still learning. As long as we seek to grow, God will show us what He has for us to learn (see Matthew 13:12 NLT).

Walking in the Kingdom is not a "name it and claim it" game. Yes, we are to believe and speak the promises, therefore we must know what they are. We then believe we have already received those promises (Mark 11:24) and trust God while we wait for those things to become evident (manifest) in our lives.

No skill is mastered in a day. If you were learning to play the piano, you would first learn the fundamentals: fingering and your scales. Then you practice the scales and the correct fingering (along with the other fundamentals) every day. You'd play the same beginner pieces of music over and over until you mastered them. As your skills grew, you'd take on more challenging music to play.

Walking in the Kingdom of God is like that. There are things to learn and practice. The more we practice, the better we get.

To access video 2, which covers chapters 4 and 5, visit crossrivermedia.com/unshakable2.

To access video 3, which covers chapters 6 and 7, visit crossrivermedia.com/unshakable3.

CHAPTER 4

FAITH AND BELIEF

Lesson 1
Our Relationship

God decided in advance to adopt us into his own family by bringing us to himself through Jesus Christ. This is what he wanted to do, and it gave him great pleasure. (Ephesians 1:5 NLT)

The No. 1 thing to remember about living in the Kingdom of God is that we are God's children. Say that with me now, out loud:

I am God's daughter/son.

Secondly, as God's children we are citizens of heaven. Say it out loud:

I am a citizen of heaven.

Did you say those statements out loud? If not, do it. Say it with conviction and then answer the following question.

How does saying those things out loud make you feel?

As you say these things, take note of what you are thinking. Do you notice a shift in your thoughts and emotions (aside from feeling a bit silly)? Write down what you noticed so you have a record to look back on and can measure your growth.

Did you feel uncomfortable or in any way negative? Examine that and determine why. If you need to, ask God why saying "I am God's daughter/son" makes you feel uneasy.

As you progress through the coming lessons, you'll be learning and developing new habits. Allow yourself the time and grace to grow. As I said earlier, this is a journey. We are not working our way into heaven or earning God's favor. We do not deserve anything God brings our way. He showers us with His grace, mercy, and blessings for Christ's sake and because He loves us!

Are you doing things in an effort to earn God's blessings? Give that some thought before you proceed. List here anything you think you might be doing in order to earn God's blessings.

Think about all the people you know. Are there some you would describe more as acquaintances than friends? Are there one or two you would describe as close friends, the kind you would confide your most intimate secrets to?

Consider the relationship you have with God at this very moment. How would you describe it?

Where does it fall on that friendship/intimacy scale?

If your relationship isn't what you'd like it to be, what change could you make starting today to improve that relationship? List at least one thing.

God desires an intimate relationship with you. Read Exodus 33:11. How does this verse describe the relationship between the Lord and Moses?

Read Jeremiah 3:20.

According to *Strong's Concordance*, the same Hebrew word translated as *friend* in Exodus 33:11 is translated as *husband* (*lover* in the NASB) in Jeremiah 3:20. Just as we have friends who know our secrets, this is the kind of intimacy God desires to have with us. Can you say with honesty that you desire this kind of intimacy with God? Why or why not?

God taught me so much as I studied the Bible and prepared to write this study. One morning during my quiet time, He brought me to the realization that my primary objective in walking fully in the Kingdom was for my benefit alone. Ouch! Selfishness is a hard truth to face about oneself. I wanted prosperity, healing, and all the other blessings God promises so my life would be easier.

God wants us to enjoy His blessings, but His primary objective is for us to share those blessings with others so Jesus can be glorified.

Stop and consider why you desire a relationship with God. Be honest with yourself, because if you aren't, you hinder your growth. Write your answer here.

Lesson 2
Faith Fundamentals

As I stated earlier, learning a new skill requires learning the fundamentals. The master players in any sport drill themselves in the fundamentals of that sport. That is how they become masters.

There are also fundamentals to God's Kingdom.

Let's examine Mark 11:20–26. We find the disciple Peter astonished to see the fig tree Jesus cursed has withered (see verses 13 and 14).

For consistency of translation, here are verses 23–25 from the NKJV: "For assuredly, I say to you, whoever says to this mountain, 'Be removed and be cast into the sea,' and does not doubt in his heart, but believes that those things he says will be done, he will have whatever he says. Therefore I say to you, whatever things you ask when you pray, believe that you receive them, and you will have them. And whenever you stand praying, if you have anything against anyone, forgive him, that your Father in heaven may also forgive you your trespasses."

Within these verses are several fundamentals of faith.

1. Believe it and speak it, "believes that those things he says will be done."

See also 2 Corinthians 4:13 and Romans 10:10.

Read the following verses and note what each person's faith did for him or her.

Matthew 9:21–22

Mark 10:51–52

Luke 17:12–19

In each of these verses Jesus says, "Your faith has made you well" (or healed you, depending on your Bible translation). "Faith is a spiritual force."[6] It makes things happen!

2. Receive it (act on it).

The original Greek for *receive* means to take. If someone was to hand you a gift, what do you have to do? You have to reach out and take it, right? Think about this for a moment. That is what we are to do in the spiritual realm as well.

But you might be asking, "How do we receive?"

FIVE STEPS FOR RECEIVING FROM GOD:[7]

1. Present the Promises
   a. Go to the Word of God and find the scriptures that fit your situation (Romans 10:17).
   b. Ask the Holy Spirit to show you the promises He desires you to apply (Romans 8:1–16).
2. Pray and Worship God
   a. Humble yourself before the Lord (James 4:10).
   b. Lay the promises before Him (1 John 5:15).
   c. Hear His wisdom and the instruction of the Holy Spirit (John 16:13).
3. Make Your Petition
   a. Write your petition out as your Word-based declaration of faith (Philippians 4:6).
   b. Present it to the High Priest of your confession, Jesus (Hebrews 3:1).
4. Prepare to Receive
   a. Let faith and patience work together in your life (James 1:3-4).

6. Kenneth Copeland

7. Kenneth Copeland, "How do I receive my healing?" http://www.kcm.org/read/questions/how-do-i-receive-my-healing, accessed 1-23-2019

5. Praise God for the Manifestation of Victory
   a. Let every request be accompanied by your thanks-
      giving to the Lord for His faithfulness to fulfill His
      promises (Philippians 4:6, 2 Corinthians 1:20).

God doesn't want ritual. If you don't follow exactly all five steps above, it doesn't mean your prayer won't be answered. As you grow in your relationship with God, the elements of praise and worship will become a natural part of your prayer life.

Now back to the faith fundamentals.

3. Forgive (Mark 11:25–26). Not forgiving others hinders your faith. See also Matthew 18:21–35.

Now it's time to make God's Word personal. Take verses specific to you and put yourself into that verse.

Here is a practical application of these fundamentals.

"Father, You are holy. I love You with all my heart, mind, soul, and strength. I praise and honor You. Without You, I can do nothing. As it says in 1 Peter 2:24, I thank You that Jesus bore all my sins and healed all my diseases. By the authority of Matthew 18:18, I command sickness to leave my body. Thank You, Father. I am healed." (Isaiah 53:5, Luke 10:19)

It's that simple. God wills that all people be saved (1 Timothy 2:4) and walk in the provision that heaven provides (2 Peter 1:3). God wants to see all His children restored to a relationship with Him. He doesn't make it hard to understand.

But it all happens by faith.

Lesson 3
Believing

Stepping out in faith is exciting and amazing. But how can we step out if we don't believe? And how can we believe if we haven't learned the truths of God's Word?

Read Mark 9:16–24. Briefly describe the events occurring in these verses.

This man had faith. Verse 18 shows us he first brought his son to the disciples for healing.

Let's look more closely at verses 22–23. "And it has often cast him into fire and into water, to destroy him. But if you can do anything, have compassion on us and help us.'

"And Jesus said to him, 'If You can'! All things are possible for one who believes" (ESV).

In verse 23 Jesus is quoting what the man said to Him, "If You can" and He's saying it in an incredulous way—that's what the exclamation point tells us. In today's language we'd say, "Well, duh! Of course, I can."

To which the man cried out, "I do believe; help my unbelief." He asked Jesus to help him where his faith was lacking. We can also ask Jesus to help us grow in our belief.

Read Luke 1:37. The NASB says, "nothing will be impossible with God." Think about only the phrase "nothing will be impossible." Stop and let those words sink deep down into your spirit.

Now turn to John 14:12. What does this say we, as believers, will do?

Don't get caught up in the verbiage "you will do greater works." Do we, as humans, have the power to perform miracles? Most certainly not. It is the power of Holy Spirit within us doing the work. (We'll take a deeper look at Holy Spirit and His power in a later chapter.)

To live strong, unshakably, in God's Kingdom, we must fully grasp that nothing is impossible for God.

Do you truly believe? Perhaps you do but wonder if He'll do it for you. This is a concern I've asked myself and heard voiced by friends.

Read the following verses and make a note about what they say about God.

Acts 10:34

Romans 2:11

What does it mean to show partiality?

What does John 15:16 say to you?

When we pray, whether for ourselves or someone else, we are activating our faith; we are trusting that God is faithful and will do according to His Word.

Lesson 4
Walking by Faith

As we begin this lesson, I want you to write down your definition of faith. Then we'll see what the Bible has to say.

Read Hebrews 11:1. How does this verse define faith?

What are the things "we hope for"?

Aren't they the promises God has given us?

Hebrews 11 is called the "Hall of Faith" because it tells us about men and women of the Old Testament and what their faith accomplished for them. When you have a few minutes, spend some time reading Hebrews 11 and chewing on what's there. For now, let's look at verse 6.

List below the three facts this verse states:

Read 1 Corinthians 2:5. Where are we to put our faith?

I used to hear people say that such-and-such didn't happen because "I didn't have enough faith." Read Luke 17:6. What does it say about the size of our faith and what it can accomplish?

There was a point in my life when I realized I was putting faith in my faith, as though it was an element completely separate from my belief. *Faith* is merely the noun we use to describe belief in, confidence in, trust in God (yes, we have faith in other things as well).

But my faith does not have the power to heal or bring about any miracles. The power to perform miracles lies in God. Faith is merely the channel for that power (like an electric cord is the channel to get electricity from the plug to the TV).

When we got saved, we had faith to believe Jesus died for our sins.

So why do so many people (myself included) struggle so much to believe all the rest of the promises?

Stop and think a moment. Do you struggle to believe God's promises? Are there particular promises in your life you want to believe, but are struggling with? List them here.

Are you trusting in your faith to bring answers to your prayers or are you trusting in God?

Read the following verses and make a short note about what they say to you.

Numbers 23:19

Joshua 21:45

Psalm 33:4

Psalm 119:90

Hebrews 10:23

2 Thessalonians 3:3

We are to put our faith in God. And though 2 Corinthians 5:7 tells us we walk by faith, it isn't a blind walk, not knowing who we trust or where we are going. It is a confident walk because we are believing and trusting in God and His promises. Faith moves us into a position to receive what God has already done.

Lesson 5
Growing Our Faith

Often our struggle to believe is a matter of lack of knowledge about God's Word or a lack of experience in that arena. For example, we struggle to believe in healing because we haven't experienced a time when God healed us.

We have to grow our faith. Remember that faith is belief, confidence, and trust in God.

But how do we grow our faith?

How do plants grow? They pull nutrients and water from the soil and soak in the sun's rays as it shines down on them.

Likewise, we need to feed our faith. What do you think we need to feed it?

Read John 6:35. What does Jesus say about himself here?

The first four books of the New Testament are also called gospels. A gospel is a record of Jesus' life and teaching. So when you are reading Matthew, Mark, Luke, or John, remember that you are reading an account of Jesus as seen from the perspective of that particular apostle.

Now let's look at John 1:1–3. Who is being called "the Word" in these verses?

Read John 1:14. What is the apostle John saying about the Word in this verse?

After having read this verse, does it change your answer to the previous question?

It might or might not have, but I want you to be clear on this point: Jesus is the Word!

The Bible is the written Word of God. In John 6:35, Jesus called Himself the bread of life. Bread is food; thus, the Bible is our main source of food for growing our faith.

How much is your growth in faith hindered by not taking in the Word? Explain your answer.

Faith also comes through experience.
Read Matthew 14:22–33. Briefly describe the events.

Most of my life I've heard preachers give Peter a hard time for his lack of faith in this passage. But who truly lacked faith here? Explain your answer.

As a disciple, Peter is known for speaking before thinking, what we often express as "putting his foot in his mouth." In this instance, he put his feet where his faith was. He put his faith into action. He stepped out of the boat!

Do you think Peter's faith grew that day? Explain your answer.

Read Luke 10:1–17. How do you suppose these disciples grew as a result of putting their faith into action?

As we end this chapter, spend some time in self-examination and answer the following questions:

What is your relationship with God like?

Are you trusting God or in money or people (or anything else) for your security?

"For we walk by faith, not by sight." 2 Corinthians 5:7 NASB

"Now all glory to God, who is able, through his mighty power at work within us, to accomplish infinitely more than we might ask or think" (Ephesians 3:20 NLT).

Chapter 5

Acting on Our Belief

Lesson 1
Hearing God

The gatekeeper opens the gate for him, and the sheep recognize his voice and come to him. He calls his own sheep by name and leads them out. (John 10:3 NLT)

Did your parents ever say to you, "Did you hear what I said?" or "Are you listening to me?"

When they said that, were they asking if you were physically able to hear the sound?

Most of you probably answered no to that.

Then what did they mean?

In the Old Testament, there is one Hebrew word used more often than any other that is translated "hear." From *Strong's Concordance*, *shâma´* means "to hear intelligently (often with implication of attention, obedience, etc.)."

The same can be said of the New Testament. One Greek word is translated "hear" the majority of times. While it does quite often refer to the faculty of hearing, it also carries with it the meaning of "pay attention, understand, learn."

Read Matthew 11:13–17.

Verse 15 states "He who has ears to hear, let him hear." The verses that follow vs. 15 expound. The people hearing did not respond to or learn from what they were hearing. When God speaks, He expects us to pay attention, learn, and obey.

List here ways of which you are aware in how God speaks to His followers.

What evidence do we have that God speaks audibly when necessary? Read the following verses. How is God's voice described?

1 Samuel 3:8

1 Kings 19:11–13

Psalm 29:3–9

John 12:28–30

I will not state that God does not speak audibly today. I've heard too many people say they audibly heard God, and who I am to deny that? However, it is not the primary method God uses to communicate today.

There is great power in spoken words, whether spoken by God or by us.

Read Genesis 1:3. What happens after God speaks?

Indeed, "God said" eight times in Genesis 1 and created our world, mankind, all that dwells on Earth, and all that exists beyond Earth.

Read the following verses. Note who is speaking and list what these verses say about the spoken word.

Isaiah 55:11

Proverbs 18:21

Romans 10:17

While the word *speak* means to utter words that can be audibly heard, it also means communicating through other ways such as written statements or other nonverbal means. A good example is an axiom mentioned in a previous lesson: Actions speak louder than words.

First and foremost, God speaks to us through His written Word, the Bible. Look up the following verses and make a quick note about what they say about the Bible.

Joshua 1:8

Romans 15:4

2 Timothy 3:16–17

But God speaks to us in other ways as well. Who is doing the speaking and teaching in the verses below?

John 14:26

John 16:13

Romans 8:26–27

2 Peter 1:20–21

Read the following verses. Through whom is God speaking?

Hebrews 1:1–2

Hebrews 13:17

Ephesians 4:11–12

God speaks through the people around us—pastors, teachers, parents, friends, and sometimes strangers.

How is God speaking to His servants in the verses below?

Genesis 37:5–10

Daniel 2:1, 9

Matthew 1:20

There are times when I wake up from a dream and know that dream was important. I've learned to ask God what it meant. I write these dreams in my journal, and often as I'm writing, God reveals the meaning.

There are dreams I had over twenty years ago that I've never forgotten. Do you think Joseph ever forgot the two dreams he had as a boy? (See Genesis 37 and 39–47 for Joseph's story.)

There are times, especially when I'm seeking an answer to a perplexing question, that I say a quick prayer as I lay down in bed and ask God to speak to me through my dreams. You can do the same.

God speaks in many ways: through His Bible, through Holy Spirit, through the people around us, and through our dreams.

How is God speaking to you at this juncture in your life?

In the next lesson we'll look at how you can be certain God speaks to you and how to recognize His voice.

Lesson 2
Learning to Recognize God's Voice

First, let's get settled in your mind and spirit that God does talk to you.

As stated in yesterday's lesson, the Bible is His #1 method.

The original languages of the Bible were Hebrew, Greek, and Aramaic. That means people have spent time translating those languages into the other languages of the world. The work of translation is not easy. Most often it isn't a word for a word, but a concept into a group of words or a single word. As discussed at the beginning of this study, English uses Lord to cover a multitude of Hebrew words that speak of God.

Ethnologue[8] reports there are 7,097 living languages in the world. According to Wikipedia, "as of October 2017 the full Bible has been translated into 670 languages, the New Testament alone into 1,521 languages and Bible portions or stories into 1,121 other languages. Thus at least some portion of the Bible has been translated into 3,312 languages." YouVersion, a mobile app for phones, has the Bible in 1,218 languages.

If you are reading a Bible, then God is speaking to you!

Since the Bible is God's primary way of speaking to us, do you think Satan likes it when people work to translate the Bible? Why or why not?

Read Romans 10:17. What does it tell us about faith?

---

8. https://www.ethnologue.com/

How do you think peoples of the world without a Bible in their language come to know Jesus Christ?

Read Mark 16:15 and Ephesians 4:11–12. What has God told us to do?

God not only speaks to us, He also speaks to others through us! No matter where in the world we live, we need to tell people about the salvation message of Jesus.

When you first meet someone how do you get to know that person?

Often, one of the first things we learn about a person is one's voice. But there's a lot more to knowing someone than just recognizing that person's voice. Besides voice, what other aspects of a person do we come to recognize as we know them better? List several here.

When it comes to better recognizing God's voice, we need to know His character. How do we come to know His character?

As we studied yesterday, God speaks in other ways besides the Bible. Let's look at a couple more verses. Read the following and note how God is speaking to us.

Psalm 19:1–2

John 12:49

Romans 1:20

Hebrews 1:2

God also speaks directly to our spirit via Holy Spirit living within us. Read the following verses:

Matthew 10:19–20

John 16:13

Romans 8:16

Read John 10:27 and think about it for a moment.

If you have accepted Jesus as Savior, then you are His sheep. And if Jesus says "my sheep hear My voice," then He is speaking to you!

What does John 10:4 say about His sheep?

As I sought to know God's voice better, I asked Him to help me. You can, too.

His direct communication often comes as random thoughts. How can we tell if that voice in our head is us, God, or Satan?

First and foremost, apply the Word to those thoughts.
- Do they agree with or violate God's Word?
- Do they encourage you to feed fleshly desires or live according to God's principles?

Discerning the still, small voice of God takes practice. He will not tell you to do something that violates His Word. Satan, on other hand, isn't likely to tell you to pray for someone.

When I'm in church and God speaks something to my spirit during worship, I still hesitate to step out and do what He's said. Plenty of times I haven't obeyed Him at all. Has this ever happened to you? If so, what stopped you?

One morning during my quiet time God called me on the carpet for failing to obey Him. I was again asking Him to speak to me and He countered with, "Why? Even when I do, you don't obey."

Another "ouch" moment with God.

Remember from yesterday's lesson that the word *hear* comes with the implication of paying attention and obeying, doing what He says. In our next lesson, we'll look at this aspect of obedience.

Lesson 3
Obeying God

If Jesus truly is the sovereign Lord of heaven and earth, then He is also the Master of our individual lives" (Charles Stanley).

Wow. Those words pierce deeply. Can we walk 100% in God's Kingdom but disobey His biblical commands and principles? Or without embracing Him as sovereign ruler over our lives? Why or why not?

You might be wondering what obeying has to do with hearing God. As a reminder, the word *hear* carries with it not just being physically able to discern sound, but also paying attention and obeying/following what is said.

Have you ever had a friend ask you for advice and then completely ignore what you told them? You're left wondering why that person even asked for help, right?

Read Isaiah 42:20. Does this describe the person above?

What good is it for someone to ask for advice if they aren't going to give it any consideration or follow that advice?

I'll be the first to admit I struggle with the word *obey*. My spirit often bristles just hearing the word. I was raised with very strict discipline. As a child when I questioned why I was to do something, the answer most often given was "Because I said so" and it was said with anger.

What is your reaction to the word *obey*?

When I became a parent myself, I more fully understood my own parents' authority. As I child I didn't. Because the words were often spoken in anger, I began to attach a negative connotation to obedience. My parents had my ultimate good at the foundation of their family rules. When they told me to do something, it was for my good. My limited view and child perspective kept me from seeing that.

We can choose to obey or not to obey what God says. Our obedience, or lack of, directly impacts the quality of our lives, but does not impact our salvation.

Let's look at how obedience impacted the Israelites. Read Exodus 23:20–21. The angel was sent to protect and guide the Israelites. What were the consequences of disobedience?

Let's take that one more step. If they refused to obey the angel's instructions, would the angel still be able to protect and guide them? Why or why not?

Back in late 2004, I got frustrated with constantly feeling discontent. My life was good, but there was something missing. I'd been walking with God for twenty-four years by then, so it wasn't that I didn't have God in my life. I didn't know what was wrong, so I began to seek answers from God.

I looked at all the things in my life that I said I valued and whether my lifestyle supported those values. I discovered I was living a life opposite of what I valued. No, I wasn't caught up in wild living. It's just that as a single mother, I had to work. I left the house at 7 a.m. and often didn't arrive back until after 5:30 p.m. I had no physical, mental, or emotional energy to share with my children.

I made a decision to move from Colorado back to the lush green and hot climate of the Nebraska/Iowa region. From the big city to a small town. I didn't make this decision lightly. But I also had not specifically heard from God to move. I began preparing my house for sale and also job searching. All this occurred over a period of eight months.

Sometime in July during my quiet time with God, He asked, "If I said no to this move, what would you do?"

In my heart, my initial response was that I'd move anyway. I came face to face with my own disobedience…again. Yes, I've had a lifetime of "ouch" moments with God.

What does Hebrews 12:6 say about how we should view our "ouch" moments?

What advice does Matthew 7:24–27 give us about obeying (following) God's principles?

Now turn to Colossians 2:20–23. What does this say about earthly principles?

Obedience isn't about performing to earn our salvation or God's approval or to prompt Him to do something for us. It's about living and walking in the best God has for us. Jeremiah 29:11 tells us God has good plans for us. He wants what He knows to be the best for our lives. (For more on what God wants for us read Deuteronomy 28:1–14.)

Read Romans 8:12–14. What guidance do these verses give about how to live?

I like Galatians 5:25 NLT, "Since we are living by the Spirit, let us follow the Spirit's leading in every part of our lives."

Remember, your citizenship lies in heaven. We may be walking around on this earth, but the principles of God's Kingdom have power over earthly principles. Following the Holy Spirit in every aspect of our lives leads to a life fully lived in the Kingdom of God.

Lesson 4
Dealing with Fear

Difficult, trying times are where our faith will be shaken. Experiencing trouble doesn't mean you are shaken in your faith. We live in a fallen world, troubles come. God uses trouble to grow our faith and our relationship with Him.

Trouble of any kind can thrust us into the world of fear—being afraid—and "what if?"

What-ifs are fears about something that hasn't happened and probably won't. Fear is a reaction to a perceived danger—real or unreal—and triggers certain chemical reactions in the body often referred to as the fight-or-flight response. The hormones released into the body prepare us to stay and fight or run away from the danger. This innate response was designed to help protect mankind from physical dangers.

For those living in Third World countries, their daily battle is to survive. For those in the Western world, today's dangers are mostly psychological—job loss, economic woes, terrorism—however, the body still chemically reacts the same.

Before going any further, let's define *fear*. *Merriam-Webster* online dictionary states this:

1 : to be afraid of : expect with alarm

2 : to have a reverential awe of

"The fear of the LORD is the beginning of wisdom" in Psalm 111:10 and Proverbs 9:10 relates to the reverential awe, not to be afraid of.

Fear, as in being afraid of, is the opposite of faith.

Read John 10:10 and 2 Timothy 1:7. If God has not given us a spirit of fear (timidity and cowardice), then where does fear come from?

Read 1 Peter 5:8. What does this say about what Satan seeks to do?

Satan wants us intimidated. He wants to defeat us and keep us cowering in the corner. Read the second half of 2 Timothy 1:7. What has God provided for us to combat the spirit of fear?

What is God telling you in the following verses?

Psalm 27:1

Psalm 34:4 (one of my personal favorites)

Psalm 46:1–2

Psalm 56:3–4

Make a list of everything God states in Isaiah 41:10–13.

When you are in the midst of trouble or a crisis, you can easily feel overwhelmed. With so much happening, even little things can become overwhelming. I've been in that situation often enough to understand that even having to make a decision about what to cook for supper can be overwhelming.

Read Isaiah 43:2–3. What is God speaking to you here?

God brought me to these verses in Isaiah specifically when I faced the crisis of my husband abusing my daughter (his step-daughter). For three years I held tightly to those verses as God walked with me through the difficulties and healing.

Read Matthew 14:22–32. Where was Peter's focus as he walked on the water? (see verse 29)

What happened when he looked at the wind and the waves?

When you face troubles, where are your thoughts focused?

If you're like I was, you tend to look at the difficulties and run down through a list of "what ifs." Fear fills us when we focus on the circumstances, and like Peter, we sink—we get entangled in fear. That's exactly where Satan wants us.

Be conscious of what you are thinking! The battle begins with our thoughts. It is our belief and trust in (our faith) and focus on God that keeps us strong.

How do the following help us conquer our fear?

Isaiah 26:3

Isaiah 54:17

John 14:1

Luke 10:19

When fear attacks, we must take action against it. What actions do the following verses advise?

James 4:7

2 Corinthians 10:5

Matthew 18:18

Read the following verses and note what they say.

Philippians 2:9–11

Romans 14:11

Jesus' name is above all names, and everything—absolutely everything—must obey the name of Jesus. God has given us power and authority over the enemy. Fear is a tool of the enemy. Just as Jesus did in His confrontation with Satan in the desert, use God's Word to fight your fear (see Matthew 4:1–11).

If you have a particular situation in your life that is a constant struggle, find verses in the Bible that promise your answer. Use those verses as you pray. We'll discuss more about spiritual warfare in a later chapter.

Read James 1:17. What does this tell us?

We do not need to be afraid of what God brings into our lives. He brings what's best for us!

As I stated at the beginning of Part 1, just because you experience a negative emotion doesn't mean your faith has been shaken. When a negative emotion assaults you, resist it, stand your ground, and fight back with the Word of God.

You are shaken only when you embrace that negative emotion and focus on the circumstances. Despite our doubts, we can choose to trust God or go with our doubts.

Knowing our identity in Christ, God's love for us, and our eternal destination will keep us unshakable during hard times.

Lesson 5
Resting in God

The concept of God's rest is another arena where there is not only a lack of knowledge, but a lot of confusion. I think part of the confusion is that there is often both a literal interpretation to God's Word as well as a spiritual interpretation.

Let's start first with the Promised Land.

Read the following verses.

Genesis 12:1–7

Exodus 3:17

Joshua 1:2–3

Hebrews 11:9

Each verse is talking about the land God promised to give to Abraham and his descendants. Today, we know it as the country of Israel, but it is often referred to as the Promised Land.

Read Exodus 33:1–14 and briefly recap what's happening.

In verse 14, what does God say He will give them?

Now let's turn our focus to *rest*.

Read Genesis 2:2–3 (the first occurrence of the word *rest*).

Explain in your own words what you see happening.

Read Exodus 23:12.

What were the Israelites instructed to do?

In today's Western world, many have lost the concept of rest—ceasing from work. We stay busy constantly, so much so that many can't even slow down their thoughts long enough to fall asleep.

Read Deuteronomy 6:10–12. What did God have ready for the Israelites as they went into the Promised Land.

They were not facing the physical work of digging wells or building houses or planting vineyards. I marvel at the fact that the houses were even full of good things, rather than empty shells infested with spiders or snakes. A far cry from their slavery in Egypt!

The Book of Joshua is about the conquest of the Promised Land. God promised them the land, but they still had to take possession of it. It's an interesting book, but for now I want to look at a few specific verses.

Read the following verses and make a brief note about each.

1:9

2:9–11

2:23–24

What did God accomplish before they ever entered the land?

Now turn to Joshua 6:1–5, 20–23.

Who went into the land before the Israelites? (see verses 22 and 23)

Who created the battle plan to conquer Jericho?

What work did the Israelites have to do?

What do the following verses promise us?

Exodus 14:14

Deuteronomy 20:4

Joshua 23:10

1 Samuel 17:47

Romans 8:31

Today, when someone accepts Jesus as Savior, we don't enter a physical promised land like the Israelites did, but we do enter a promised land—the Kingdom of God!

What do the following verses say to you?

Matthew 11:28–30

John 14:27

When you are at peace with something are you worried? Why or why not?

Before I accepted Christ as Lord, I was constantly trying to figure out how to do life—figure out relationships, how to earn a living, how to be a good wife.

After accepting Jesus, I had His Spirit within me to lead the way. I had the Bible to teach me about being a wife, how to handle finances, and more. Just as God provided the battle plans to Joshua, He provides us with what we need to know—as long as we seek Him and ask.

Has anyone ever said to you, "Give it to me and I'll take care of it"? If so, did you continue to try to figure out the problem or did you trust and rest that it would be done?

For us to rest in God is to trust He will fulfill His promises. That means when we pray about something, we do not worry or fret or attempt to solve the problem in our own strength. We rest and trust in God's ability.

Read Hebrews 4:8–10.

These verses describe our final rest, when we cease from all our labor and leave this earth for heaven—the true Promised Land.

> *"I will look up to the mountains—does my help come from there? My help comes from the LORD, who made heaven and earth!" (Psalm 121:1–2 NLT)*

> *"Give your burdens to the LORD, and he will take care of you. He will not permit the godly to slip and fall." (Psalm 55:22 NLT)*

CHAPTER 6

OUR AUTHORITY/POWER

Lesson 1
Our Authority and Power

Behold! I have given you authority and power to trample upon
serpents and scorpions, and [physical and mental strength
and ability] over all the power that the enemy [possesses]; and
nothing shall in any way harm you. (Luke 10:19 AMPCE)

Knowing our authority in the Kingdom is as essential as knowing our identity. So let's do a brief review of our identity. John 1:12, Romans 8:16, and Ephesians 1:5 tell us we are God's children through Christ. We are princesses or princes. Royalty!

Ephesian 6:20 identifies us as ambassadors for Christ. Ambassadors represent their country and carry the authority of that country. As ambassadors for Christ, we have His authority, but you don't need to take my word for it. Let's find that authority in the Word.

Matthew 16:19
Matthew 18:18
Matthew 28:18–20

Luke 9:1

Luke 10:19

God does not send us into the world without His authority. Neither does He send us into the world without His power. Read the following verses.

Luke 24:49

Acts 1:8

Ephesian 3:16

2 Timothy 1:7

Now let's take a closer look at Matthew 16:19.

Jesus begins by saying, "I will give you the keys to the kingdom of Heaven."

What do keys do?

What two things does He name as keys?

To bind is to tie up. To loose is to untie. The keys He has given us allow us to forbid (bind) or permit (loose). We want to bind the devil and his cohorts, and to loose the power of God, be it Holy Spirit or His ministering angels.

Next, we'll look more closely at the power God gives us.

Lesson 2
Baptized and Filled with the Holy Spirit

As human beings we are very limited in power. And I am so glad God doesn't expect or want us to operate from our own human power. So let's take a look at the power God does provide and how He provides it.

Perhaps you've heard the phrase "being baptized in the Spirit." But this phrase is often a source of confusion. What do you think it means?

Read the following verses.

Matthew 3:11

Mark 1:8

From *Strong's Concordance* the original Greek word used here for *baptize* means "to immerse, submerge; to make whelmed (i.e. fully wet); wash."

When John the Baptist was baptizing people, he stood in the river (or the sea) along with the penitent and fully submerged that person into the water. This outward physical act represented the act of being cleansed of sin. John's baptism is known as the baptism of repentance (see Acts 19:4). The people were repenting of only their sins, not embracing Jesus as Savior.

The Jew of that day understood *clean* and *unclean*. It was a part of the Law (see Exodus 30:17–21). The Book of Leviticus is filled with verse after verse about what was unclean, the consequences of being unclean, and the requirement to once again be ceremonially clean. The priests had to wash prior to offering any sacrifice or entering the tabernacle.

Now read the following verses and write what it says about the Holy Spirit.

Acts 2:38

1 Corinthians 6:19

2 Corinthians 1:21–22

Now go to Acts 19:1–5 and give a brief account of what happens in these verses.

We are baptized, immersed, into the body of Christ by Holy Spirit when we accept Christ as Savior.

Read John 20:1–22. What happens here and when?

In the days of the Old Testament, Holy Spirit did not reside within (indwell) a person. Holy Spirit came upon a person at a certain time for a certain event. This moment in John 20 was the moment Holy Spirit came to indwell the disciples. For the disciples, it was their Acts 2:38 moment.

Today, the physical act of baptism (whether fully immersed or not) is an outward symbol of our acceptance as Christ as Lord, but the act of baptism itself does not bring salvation.

"Being filled with the Holy Spirit" is another phrase we often hear. In my years as a born-again Christian, I've heard many preachers teach and speak these two phrases as though they were synonymous—the same. They are not!

Read Acts 2:1–4. What day is it?

Pentecost is the Greek word for the Jewish festival called Feast of Weeks. It was celebrated fifty days after Passover.

Read John 20:11–22.

Now contrast the day in Acts 2:4 with the day in John 20:21. Are they the same days?

Read Acts 2:4 again. Does the verse say they were *baptized* with the Holy Spirit or *filled* with the Holy Spirit?

To you, what is the difference between being baptized (washed) and being filled?

There are two distinct actions occurring in John 20:21 and in Acts 2:4. Here is *Strong's* definition of the original Greek word used in Acts 2:4: "to 'fill' (literally or figuratively (imbue, influence, supply))."

Read Acts 2:5–41.

What initially happened? (see vss. 4 and 6)

From verse 14 to 40, the apostle Peter preached his first sermon! The very same Peter who only days earlier had three times denied Jesus. This filling of the Holy Spirit supplies us with the power of Holy Spirit and enables us to function through that power.

As we learned in the previous lesson, the apostle Paul tells us in Ephesians 5:18 to be filled with the Holy Spirit. Do you think that filling is a one-time event or does it occur more often? Why or why not?

What does Ephesians 5:18 discourage, and what does it encourage?

Being filled with the Spirit is an event that occurs more than once. And we can ask for this filling power of the Holy Spirit whenever we need it!

Lesson 3
Speaking in Tongues

Speaking in tongues is a topic many preachers avoid. But we do so at our peril because it is a vital means of spiritual growth as well as a spiritual weapon.

First and foremost, I do not want this aspect of life in Christ to create division. Many say speaking in tongues was for a day long past. But Jesus is the same yesterday, today, and forever (Hebrews 13:8).

Read 1 Corinthians 14:18. Did Paul speak in tongues?

On the Day of Pentecost when Peter and the other disciples spoke in tongues, were they speaking a language that no one understood? See Acts 2:8–11.

What does 1 Corinthians 14:2 say about speaking in tongues?

Speaking in tongues is the language of the Spirit, a private prayer language that goes straight to God. A direct line to God that the devil can't understand or interfere with!

Read Isaiah 55:11. What does this say about God's word?

Do you think that whatever is spoken in the Spirit falls in the realm of Isaiah 55:11? Why or why not?

Read the following and list what Holy Spirit provides for us.

Acts 1:8

Romans 8:26–27

Read James 1:17. What God brings our way is good and for our good. That includes the gift of speaking in tongues.

If you are hesitant about this, examine your reasons. Yes, it's hard for our mind (our intellect) to fathom. This language completely bypasses the mind.

Does it make you feel foolish? I felt that way when I first began speaking in tongues. But don't refuse this just because you'll feel foolish or be embarrassed. It is a gift from God you can choose to accept or not.

Read 1 Corinthians 14:4. What does this say about speaking in the Spirit?

Drop down to verse 15. How does it encourage us to pray?

Read Ephesians 6:18. The apostle Paul includes praying in the Spirit in his discussion of our spiritual armor. Given what you have learned about praying in tongues, how do you see it as a part of our spiritual armor?

I cannot begin to tell you how much has changed in my life since I started praying in tongues every day, during every moment my brain isn't engaged (you know, while washing dishes or traipsing off to get the mail). New revelation comes as I read and study the Bible, my confidence and faith in God is growing in leaps and bounds. I hear God's voice more clearly.

Do not be afraid of this mighty gift!

Lesson 4
God's Promises

The word *promise* occurs fifty-three times in fifty verses in the King James Bible. But there are thousands of promises God has made in the Bible. A Google search reveals sites that state various numbers: over 3000, 5467, 7487. I'm not going to limit His Word by trying to count them. What speaks to one person as a promise for the situation might not speak the same way to another.

One thing is for sure about God's promises. Read 2 Corinthians 1:20 and list what it says.

Remember God cannot lie; He cannot go back on His Word. He is in covenant with Jesus, and we are in covenant with Jesus. If God didn't fulfill His promises, He would be breaking His covenant. (Review chapters 1 and 2 as needed.)

His Word is the foundation we stand on when in Ephesians 6:13 the apostle Paul tells us "having done all, to stand."

Now let's dive in and look at two amazing things, among the many, God has provided for our faith walk.

Read 2 Peter 1:3–4.

What does verse 3 say we have been given?

How do we access that? (look at the second half of the verse)

Depending on your translation, verse 4 tells us God's promises are exceeding great, great, very great; precious; magnificent.

What else does this verse tell us about God's promises?

Through His promises we actually become partners with God. We share His divine nature through His promises.

When Holy Spirit brought that revelation to me about this verse, I could have jumped for joy. We do not "become gods," but His power and nature flow into and through us via Holy Spirit as that nature/power connects with our faith in God's promises.

Read Ephesians 1:17–20. I often pray verses 17 and 18 for myself and others.

What power raised Jesus from the dead?

Does that same power reside within us?

Does God provide meagerly or abundantly? Read 2 Corinthians 9:8 and Ephesians 3:20.

If we didn't have His Word, how could we know what God can and will do for us? Explain your answer.

Read Romans 4:16-21.

What does verse 19 say about Abraham's faith?

What two things does verse 20 tell us about Abraham?

Finally, what does verse 21 tell us?

Abraham did not waver through unbelief but was fully convinced God was able to perform what He had promised. We also must be fully convinced God is able and will perform His promises. These very promises are the basis for our prayers.

Lesson 5
The Power of Praise

I struggled with where to place this lesson. Praise is powerful, and when we are fighting a tough battle, praise can give us the focus we need and strength to battle on.

Merriam Webster's Online Dictionary defines praise as "to express a favorable judgment of : commend; to glorify (a god or saint) especially by the attribution of perfections."

In praising God, our focus is on Him and all He does and has done for us and for others. Let's examine some of the praises given us in the Bible.

Turn to the Book of Psalms. A psalm is a poem set to music. Psalms has 150 of them. We lose much of their beauty in translation, and we don't have the music they were originally sung to. Let's look at several verses. Make a note of what stands out to you.

7:17

9:11

21:13

28:7

35:28

47:1 (yes, it's okay to clap your hands to God in church)

63:4 (again, it's okay to raise your hands in praise at church)

All of Psalm 150

How important do you think praise is to God?

Let's examine something that on the surface looks totally unrelated to praise.

Read Numbers 2:2–3. Where was the tribe of Judah to set up camp?

An important note here about the tabernacle (tent of meeting in some translations): the only entrance was on the east side.

This chapter outlines where each tribe of Israel was to set up camp as they traversed the desert, and how they were to break camp as well. Now turn to Numbers 2:9. What does this verse say about the tribe of Judah?

Now turn to Judges 1:1–2 and 20:18. Who was to go first?

Read Genesis 49:8–10. What is occurring in these verses?

A scepter and ruler's staff are symbols of authority and sovereignty. Judah and his descendants are tremendously important.

Read Revelation 5:5. Who is this referring to?

I know, I know. You're wondering what all this has to do with praise. The name Judah means "let Him (God) be praised."

When you link all these things together you get an amazing picture! Judah camped on the east side of the tabernacle, in front of the only entrance. Jesus is the Lion of Judah. He described Himself as the doorway (see John 10:9). Praise is a doorway to God!

We can plumb the depths of God's Word and find new revelations until the day He calls us home to heaven!

Now let's look at a passage that shows us the battle-fighting power of praise. Read 2 Chronicles 20:15–28.

Who went out first as they headed to the battle? (vs. 21)

What happened as they began to praise? (vs. 22)

Did the men have to fight any battles?

When they returned to Jerusalem, what were they doing?

They went out praising and they returned praising!

I've noticed many people meander into church during, and quite often after, our time of praise and worship. It breaks my heart to see this. Praise is a time for us to express to God our love for Him. My intent in praise is to give back to Him, but as often happens, He ministers to me as well. We miss so much of what God has for us when we don't offer Him our praise.

I hope after reading this lesson you'll view praise and worship time at church in a new light: as ministry to God, but also as a weapon of warfare.

Chapter 7

Our Weapons and Armor

Lesson 1
Satan's Tactics

The thief does not come except to steal, and to kill, and to destroy. (John 10:10a NKJV)

In an earlier chapter, I made a point of the power of the spoken word. I sometimes pray silently, but most of the time I speak my requests out loud. And if there's one thing I've learned about prayer, it is to pray God's Word—it is our sword but also our belt of truth spoken of in Ephesians 6.

In all we do, our wisest example is Jesus. Let's examine how He responded when Satan attacked him. Read Matthew 4:1–11.

Jesus has been in the desert for forty days and forty nights, fasting (doing without food) the whole time. Jesus was fully man during His time here on Earth. Now imagine His state of well-being as he reached the fortieth day.

Enter Satan, with a head-on assault.

What are Satan's first words to Jesus? (vs. 3)

Does Jesus respond to that accusation? (vs. 4)

Twice Satan says, "If You are the Son of God...". Why do you suppose Jesus never responds to those words?

While on earth Jesus functioned as fully human, with the power of Holy Spirit working through Him. Satan knew Jesus is the Son of God, but at that moment, he was tempting Jesus to set aside His humanity and pick up His deity.

Had Jesus done this, it would have thwarted the plan of salvation—Jesus dying to pay the price for mankind's salvation.

Jesus knew exactly what He had come to do and wasn't going to get into a debate with the devil about it. Following Christ's example, we shouldn't debate with the devil either. So let's take a look at how Jesus *did* respond.

Where does Satan aim his first attack? (vs. 3)

And how does Jesus respond?

In verse 6, how does Satan attack Jesus?

What was Satan attempting to do?

How does Jesus respond?

Three times Satan tempts Jesus, and three times Jesus rebukes Satan with the truth of God's written word.

Satan is not omniscient (all knowing). That means he doesn't know our thoughts. Neither is he omnipresent (present everywhere). He can't be everywhere in the world all at once. But his strategy includes striking us over and over and over and over until he penetrates our mind.

He works to deceive us by making us
- doubt our position in Christ,
- doubt the truth of God's Word,
- and doubt God.

Read 1 John 2:16. In what three areas does Satan aim his attacks at us?

God has not left us defenseless! Read the following verses. What has God given us for the battle?

Matthew 10:1

Luke 9:1

Luke 10:19

Mark 3:14–15

Ephesians 6:10–18

What do the following verses say concerning our battle?

Isaiah 54:17

Romans 8:37

1 John 4:4

But here is the best part. Read the following verses and write down what they tell us about Satan.

Colossians 2:15

Revelation 12:10

Hebrews 2:14–15

Satan is a defeated foe! He can only be successful if we are not grounded in the truth of God's written Word, the Bible, which is referred to as the sword of the Spirit in Ephesians 6:17. Our most important weapon against Satan is the Bible. (In later lessons we'll look at additional items God has provided for the battle.)

"The only place that rightfully belongs to the devil is the small space of ground that is right underneath your feet" (Rick Renner). (See Genesis 3:14–15 and Deuteronomy 28:13.)

Read James 4:7–8. What does verse 7 promise?

Verse 8?

Second Corinthians 10:4–5 tell us, "For the weapons of our warfare *are* not carnal but mighty in God for pulling down strongholds, casting down arguments and every high thing that exalts itself against the knowledge of God, **bringing every thought into captivity to the obedience of Christ**" (NKJV, emphasis mine).

Every day I become more and more convinced there is a Bible verse to counteract any thought that doesn't line up with God's Word. Jesus used the written Word to respond to Satan's attacks. We should, too!

If you are battling a particular issue, ask the Lord to lead you to specific verses that speak His truth about that issue. Pray those verses daily and stand on that promise.

Lesson 2
Our Armor

God has provided for our protection, and the apostle Paul outlines that for us. Read Ephesians 6:10–18. Paul has written this passage using the Roman soldier as an analogy. There is no doubt that the Jew and Gentile of Jesus' day and Paul's day knew well the power, strength, and weaponry of the Roman soldier.

Let's examine this passage verse by verse beginning with verse 13, a verse often misunderstood and taught incorrectly.

Let's look specifically at "having done all, to stand."

Many see this as when you've done everything you know how to do, you just grin and bear it.

What is the "all" we are supposed to be doing?

The Greek from *Strong's Concordance* for "having done" means "to work fully, i.e. accomplish; by implication, to finish."

A better translation of this verse comes from the New Living Translation: "Therefore, put on every piece of God's armor so you will be able to resist the enemy in the time of evil. Then after the battle you will still be standing firm."

Paul starts this discussion of our armor by telling us we'll come through the battle not bloodied and defeated, but victorious. God's Word is powerful. Romans 8:37 tells us we are more than conquerors.

Now let's look at our armor and weapons.

Vs. 14: gird your waist with truth (or depending on your translation, put on the belt of truth).

The loin belt was the most important piece for the Roman

soldier. It held all the other pieces in place. It did not just wrap around his waist, but it provided protection for his loins. It held the breastplate in place, and had places to hold his sword, lance, and shield.

Today's application: put on truth as we would a belt around our waist so we are prepared for any attack and aren't caught unaware. We need to know the truths of the Bible so we can recognize Satan's lies. We want to keep ourselves strong with truth at all times.

Read John 1:1, 14 and 14:6.

What do these verses tell us about truth?

Our Bible is our belt of truth! "The word of God is central and foremost to everything else that we have in God" (Rick Renner, *Dressed to Kill*).

Back to vs. 14: "put on the breastplate of righteousness." A breastplate protects our vital organs. While we are inclined to think the breastplate covers only the front, the breastplate of the Roman soldier covered both the front and the back. We can't see an attack from behind, but our breastplate protects our back as well as our front.

Read Proverbs 4:23. What does this tell us to do?

The writer isn't speaking about the physical heart, but about our inner man, the seat of our moral character, our emotions, and passions.

According to the verses below, where does our righteousness come from?

1 Corinthians 1:30

2 Corinthians 5:21

Philippians 3:9

Vs. 15: "shod your feet with the preparation of the gospel of peace."

A Roman soldier wore greaves, a tube-like piece of bronze or brass that covered his leg from his knee to his ankle.[9] The upper portion of his shoe was leather and the sole held hob nails. These nails allowed him to have sure footing on any ground, but also served as a weapon. He stopped for nothing and no one, and whatever got under his feet was stomped through with those hob nails.

All sounds rather gory, I know. Helps us understand why the Jewish feared the Romans the way they did.

Read Ephesians 6:12 and list the enemies named here.

What does God say about us and Satan? Read Genesis 3:15 and Romans 16:20.

9. Rick Renner, *Dressed to Kill*

Read Ephesians 2:14, Isaiah 9:6, and Philippians 4:7.
What do these verses tell us?

The armor, especially God's peace, will help us stand unshakable and immovable in our faith. The peace of God will
guard your heart and mind.

Lesson 3
Our Armor, cont'd

Today, we'll continue our look at Ephesians 6:10–18. If necessary, reread those verses.

In verse 16 we discover "the shield of faith."

The Roman soldier's shield was made especially for him, fitted to his measurements. It wasn't that tiny little round thing we so often see in the movies. No, it was oblong and more the size of a door. It shielded his entire body, which is why it was specially made for him. No "one size fits all" for the Roman soldier.

What did God give us according to Romans 12:3?

What does our faith shield do for us? See Ephesians 6:16.

The verse doesn't say we can stop *some* of Satan's arrows. No, it says *all*. I love that!

But what are we to have faith in? Read Galatians 2:16, 20 and Romans 3:22.

Vs. 17: "take the helmet of salvation." The human being is a spirit with a soul that lives within a body. Our mind, will, and emotions reside within our soul. The mind utilizes the brain to think, reason, and conclude. The mind is where we fight our spiritual battles.

The helmet of the Roman soldier covered not only his head, but also the back of his neck—a prime target for the battle axe.

Where does our salvation lie? Read 2 Corinthians 5:15 and Acts 4:10–12.

Moving further into verse 17. Take the "sword of the Spirit which is the word of God." A sword is not a tool for defense, but for offense. Our sword is the Word of God—the Bible.

In the original Greek, *word* is *rhema*. *Vine's Expository Dictionary* explains rhema this way: "The reference is not to the whole Bible as such, but to the individual verses that the Spirit brings to our remembrance for use in time of need, a prerequisite being the regular storing of the mind with Scripture."

Remember during Jesus' time in the desert, He used the written Word against Satan. These were verses Holy Spirit brought to Jesus' remembrance as He battled Satan in that moment. Holy Spirit does the same for us, but note the prerequisite. He can't help us remember something we haven't read.

Now look at Ephesians 6:18. Do you consider praying in the Spirit as God's Word? Why or why not?

Within the covers of the written Word are all the answers and words you need to fight the enemy and walk victoriously, unshakably in God's Kingdom.

Read Isaiah 55:11. We've read this verse several times in various lessons. When we speak the Word of God in faith, it accomplishes its task. Has this truth begun to take root in your heart? Why or why not?

Read John 17:17, then John 1:1, 14. What do these say?

Have these verses brought you any new revelation about Jesus? If so, what?

Through all the verses we have examined and compared to our spiritual armor, we've discovered that Jesus doesn't just have the answers to our problems and needs, He *is* the answer.

The Bible is our source of life and our weapon for battle. You are fodder in the hands of Satan if you do not spend time reading God's Word!

Lesson 4
Our Prayers

W hat a Friend we have in Jesus" is a hymn I used to sing in church in years past. Here is verse 1.

"What a Friend we have in Jesus,
All our sins and griefs to bear!
What a privilege to carry
Everything to God in prayer!
O what peace we often forfeit,
O what needless pain we bear,
All because we do not carry
Everything to God in prayer!"

Prayer is often the last thing we do when facing troubles, but it should be the first. Next to the Word of God, prayer is our most powerful weapon!

What does the above hymn tell us happens because we don't take everything to God in prayer?

What does 1 Peter 5:7 admonish us to do?

Many people misunderstand what prayer is. Simply, it is a dialog with God. It's not complicated and can take place anywhere—in church, in the shower, as you wash the supper dishes, in the car on the way to work. A prayer can be one sentence and last five seconds, or last all day long.

When you converse with a friend, are you the one doing all the talking? Of course not. Since prayer is a dialog with God, that means we also stop and listen for Him to speak to us. (If needed, reread the lessons on hearing from God.)

Read the following verses and make a note of the two specific things these verses state.

Romans 10:10

2 Corinthians 4:13

One of the fundamentals of faith is to believe in our heart and then to speak.

John 15:7 NKJV says: "If you abide in Me, and My words abide in you, you will ask what you desire, and it shall be done for you."

Strong's Concordance tells us *abide* means "to stay (in a given place, state, relation or expectancy):—abide, continue, dwell, endure, be present, remain, stand, tarry (for)." I think we get better at abiding as our relationship with God grows.

As I've said before, God is not a genie, and prayer is not a "name it, claim it" strategy. An important part of John 15:7 is "my words abide in you." If you aren't reading the Bible, it's unlikely that Jesus' words are abiding in you.

Now read James 4:3 and 1 John 5:14. Note below what critical elements for prayer they contain.

Look up the following verses and make notes on what each verse says to you.

Hebrews 11:6

James 1:6

Matthew 9:22

Matthew 15:28

Mark 10:52

Luke 17:19

Having faith is essential not only in your walk with God, but in receiving answers to your prayers!

What does 2 Corinthians 1:20 say about God's promises?

We've looked at this verse before. The promises spoken of here are those in His Word. Seek His wisdom, His plan for you. Seek His promises and know His Word. Base your prayers on His promises because He cannot say no to His own promises.

What many of us struggle with is waiting for the answer to reach the physical realm. What do the following verses tell us to employ?

Hebrews 10:36

James 5:7

Read Colossians 4:2. What three things does this verse tell us to do?

Read Philippians 4:6–7. What attitude are we to carry with us as we pray? (vs. 6)

What benefit, besides our answers, comes with our prayers? (vs. 7)

Don't spend time telling Jesus the problem. He knows all things! He knows what you need before you ask (Matthew 6:8).

Prayer asks God to take action on our behalf for the sake of Christ—because He died on the cross for us to procure those promises and what heaven has! "You can ask for anything in my name, and I will do it, so that the Son can bring glory to the Father" (John 14:13 NLT). We pray in Jesus' name because He instructed us to. God answers prayer because of what Christ did, not because of anything we do.

Prayer is one of the ways God established to accomplish His will here on earth. He acts when someone somewhere asks Him in faith to do something.

Turn to 1 John 5:14–15 and describe in your own words what these verses tell us.

"God cannot turn away from your petition when it's based on His Word" (Kenneth Copeland).

Lesson 5
Prayer, cont'd

As stated in an earlier chapter, the power of death and life are in the tongue (Proverbs 18:21). First God spoke, then the physical world emerged.

Everything in the natural realm first starts in the supernatural with a vision. Prayer is the next step. First we see the answer to our prayers in our mind, then through our words of faith, the answer comes forth in the natural realm. Prayer is the foundation. Success happens first in our prayers.

Sometimes we simply haven't got the right words to pray. As we learned earlier, Jesus used the written Word to rebuke Satan.

Read the following verses and write down what each one tells us about God's Word.

Hebrews 4:12

2 Timothy 3:16–17

Have you ever prayed a specific verse and inserted your name or the name of a loved one into the verse? Doing that is personalizing the verse to you and your situation. Praying Scripture is more powerful than using your own words because the Bible is God's Word, God-breathed and Holy Spirit-inspired. Read Isaiah 55:10–11. Restate in your own words what they say.

In light of this fact about God's Word, how will this impact your prayers?

When we have no words to pray, who can pray for us? Read Romans 8:26.

Read Mark 11:20–24. What is the key element to our prayers? (See the last half of verse 23.)

What does verse 24 tell us to do concerning our prayers?

Do you struggle with believing you have already received the answer to your prayer? Why or why not?

Sometimes it seems our prayers go unanswered—maybe it feels more often than sometimes. Let's look at some possible reasons our prayers might be hindered.

Look at Mark 11:23 again. What does it tell us not to do?

Read Mark 11:25. Can unforgiveness hinder our prayers? Why or why not?

What does James 4:3 have to say?

Read Matthew 21:22. It isn't always easy to believe you'll receive what you ask for. What does Mark 9:24 tell us we can do?

Read 1 Peter 3:7. How does this verse caution husbands?

If we are praying for something but speaking the opposite to those around us, how does that affect our prayers? Consider Proverbs 18:21 as you write your answer.

When it comes to hindrances to our prayers, we must also remember there are spiritual powers that attempt to stop God's answers from getting to us. Read Daniel 10:1–13.

What did the angel tell Daniel concerning his prayer? (vs. 12)

How long did the angel battle before the angel Michael came to help?

Know that when you seek to walk 100% in the Kingdom of God, the devil won't be happy. He's going to work hard to defeat you, to make you doubt God and all that He promises.

What do the following verses say about our prayers.

Psalm 55:17

Psalm 66:18–20

Psalm 91:15–16

What does 1 Thessalonians 5:17 tell us to do?

Do you think it's possible to pray without ceasing? Why or why not?

Make a list of the things you've been praying for.

Now find a promise from God that is the foundation for each of your prayers and next to each item write the Bible verse(s) that promises the answer. Speak this out loud and believe. Do not look at your present circumstances. Believe you have received!

Read 1 Thessalonians 5:24. How does this encourage you concerning your prayers?

Read Ephesian 3:20 and Luke 1:37.
Is anything too hard for God?

Remember, you are in covenant with God, and God is faithful to perform His promises—otherwise He would be breaking His covenant.

Lesson 6
Doing Battle

Troubles come because we live in a fallen, sinful world. Most people don't like having troubles. I know I don't. What do the following verses say about trouble?

James 1:2

John 16:33

What does Romans 8:28 promise those who love God?

We have two choices when difficulties come our way: to trust God to bring us through it or to turn away from Him.

Go back to James 1:2, but now read verses 3 and 4 as well.

God allows difficulties to help us grow in our faith, to refine us, and conform us to the image of His Son.

Read Ephesians 6:12 again. In our lesson on our armor, you listed the enemies you are battling against. But God has not left us to do battle on our own.

Read Exodus 14:14 and 2 Chronicles 20:15.

In these verses who fights our battles?

Our part is to trust God and have faith that He will do what He said He would. (Review the lesson on promises if needed.)

As I was studying and listening to teaching on prayer, God showed me an amazing thing. Let me expound.

Read Ephesians 6:18. We looked at this verse in earlier lessons. Is praying in tongues God's word? (To find your answer, ask who is doing the praying.)

Is the Holy Spirit God?

The answer to those questions is yes!

Read the following verses. The same two things are happening in these verses. What are they?

Romans 10:10

Mark 11:23–24

2 Corinthians 4:13

We believe, and we speak.

How did God create the world? Genesis 1:3 tells us "God said," not God thought or imagined, but *said*. He spoke.

Now let's take yet another look at Isaiah 55:11 and I'll pull this all together.

This verse tells us that God's Word always accomplishes what it is sent forth to do. In Exodus 14:14 and 2 Chronicles 20:15 we learned that God fights our battles.

So how is it that God fights our battles? Through His Word!

Who is speaking in the following verses?

Luke 4:8

Matthew 16:23

Mark 4:35–41

In all things, Jesus is our model. If He spoke, then we also must speak.

I want to caution you here. If you state in your morning prayers "By Jesus stripes I am healed," and then all day long say to everyone you see "I am so sick," what have you done with your words?

Like a refund cancels a purchase, our negative words cancel our positive words. Watch what you say out loud and to yourself.

God has provided our armor (Jesus!) and His Word. He has provided all we need! And further He has told us in His Word that He fights our battles.

Our part is to believe Him, have faith, and speak His Word, be it His written Word or through praying in the Spirit.

Our toughest battle is one of the mind. Believing Him. Read 2 Corinthians 10:3–5 again. What does vs. 5 tell us to do with our thoughts?

How do we take our thoughts captive? Read Romans 12:2.

Ephesians 4:22–24 NLT tell us: "Throw off your old sinful nature and your former way of life, which is corrupted by lust and deception. Instead, let the Spirit renew your thoughts and attitudes. Put on your new nature, created to be like God— truly righteous and holy."

Living fully in God's Kingdom with unshakable faith might seem impossible. But with God ALL THINGS ARE POSSIBLE! Here are some final verses to encourage you.

Deuteronomy 1:30

Deuteronomy 20:4

Isaiah 54:17

Jeremiah 1:19

James 4:7–8

1 John 5:4

Revelation 12:11

Know that Satan isn't going to like that you are digging deeper into the Bible and seeking to grow strong in God. But also know that God is fighting for you.

If you haven't read much of the Bible before, I encourage you to start with the Book of John. After that, read Ephesians. It is filled with what it means to live in the Kingdom.

If you could sign up to receive a text message from God every day, would you? The Bible is His Word to us. There are websites and apps that offer daily doses of the Word. Sign up for one and receive God's Word every day as you grow in your relationship with Him and in your walk of unshakable faith.

Believe. Trust. Speak His promises.

"What you think is your worst moment is your biggest moment to lean on Him." (Cindi Lombardo, That's My God*)*

LEADER GUIDE

Note: Individual study books of Unshakable Faith *can be purchased at a discount with orders of five (5) or more, shipped to one place. Available to US residents only. Contact deb@ crossrivermedia.com to order.*

This is your study. Make it such. This guide is intended for that purpose alone—to guide you, not dictate how it's done.

Each week's lesson includes questions for potential discussion. Choose as you see fit. If you ask a question, but no one is willing to share, move on to another. In time, as the group gets more comfortable with each other, this should change. Each chapter has been designed to be completed in one week. However, in group study this can be stretched to suit your group and allow for more in-depth discussion of the chapter topics. If you chose to do this, pick a few questions from the general discussion and supplement them with those under DIVING DEEPER. Questions are meant to help you get started. Don't hesitate to pose your own!

Allow time to wrap up the discussion and have closing prayer. Take note of struggles expressed so needs can be addressed in prayer.

There are three videos that accompany this group Bible study. Video 1 is to be viewed at your first meeting and introduces part 1. Video 2 introduces part 2. Video 3 expounds on chapters 6 and 7.

Link to video 1: crossrivermedia.com/unshakable1. Allow approximately eight minutes to view the video at the beginning of class.

Link to video 2: crossrivermedia.com/unshakable2. Allow approximately five minutes to view the video at the beginning of the class.

Link to video 3: crossrivermedia.com/unshakable3. Allow approximately seven minutes to view the video at the beginning of the class.

WEEK ONE

First meeting: Open with prayer and invite the Holy Spirit into your meeting. Allow a brief time for introductions and getting acquainted. Establish group procedures, what lessons of each chapter will be covered each week, who will lead the meetings, the time, place, and dates.

To encourage open discussion, stress that what is shared in the group stays in the group. Proverbs 16:28b "gossip separates the best of friends." Be patient as the group establishes trust in one another.

DISCUSSION QUESTIONS
Living in God's Kingdom means God rules our lives. Are you living by God's rules or are you controlling your life? (If needed, explain we aren't living those rules in order to earn salvation, but simply in obedience to God because He knows what's best for us.)

Do you struggle to believe God loves you unconditionally? If so, are you willing to share why? Perhaps discuss how God expresses His love to you personally.

How familiar were you with the names of God? Was there one or two that stood out to you and why?

What attribute of God was new to you or is a favorite? Was there a verse that brought new revelation?

Would anyone like to share their answer to "How has your perception of God changed?" considering what you learned in this chapter?

What lesson in this chapter spoke the most to you and why?

DIVING DEEPER (TWO WEEKS PER CHAPTER)
Chose a few questions from the general discussion questions above and supplement them with these or your own.

LESSONS 1-3

How do you feel about David's statement in Psalm 16:8 NASB, "I have set the LORD continually before me; Because He is at my right hand, I will not be shaken"? How can we achieve that?

Discuss how our earthly fathers affect our perception of God. Ask if anyone is willing to share his/her struggle, then spend time reviewing several of the verses in Lessons 2 and 3 that speak to the need.

LESSONS 4-6

Discuss attributes of God that were new to participants. How does knowing about that attribute impact their faith in God?

How does understanding God's grace, mercy, and love for us impact how we live our lives?

CLOSE WITH PRAYER. Address any issues or needs expressed during discussion.

WEEK TWO

Open with prayer and invite the Holy Spirit into your meeting. If new members have joined, allow for a brief introduction.

DISCUSSION QUESTIONS

After reading Lesson 1, did anyone discover they've been operating under the Law of the Covenant? Would you be willing to share?

Review and discuss the chart on page 41, the contrast of the covenant of the law and covenant of grace from Creflo Dollar.

As a child of the King, you are either a princess or prince. How does thinking of yourself as royalty make you feel?

Satan's only tool is deception. Read out loud and discuss 2 Corinthians 10:3–5 and how to put it into practice.

Discuss 1 John 4:18. Refer to the Amplified Bible version on page 48 (middle of Lesson 5) to guide the discussion.

Discuss what it means to be an ambassador for our country. How does that relate to being ambassadors for Christ? Do people expect certain things from those they know to be Christ followers?

What lesson in this chapter spoke the most to you and why?

DIVING DEEPER (TWO WEEKS PER CHAPTER)

Chose a few questions from the general discussion questions above and supplement them with these or your own.

LESSONS 1–3

Discuss God's blessing—available to all believers through Christ—that is named in Deuteronomy 28:1–13. How does knowing this blessing is available to you impact you?

Review the Bible verses on page 42 (beginning of Lesson 3) and discuss the transformation that occurs during salvation—God removing the old nature and giving us a new nature.

LESSONS 4–6

Share your own story of how God was faithful in a particular circumstance. Ask others to share their stories.

Discuss how our behavior impacts our witness about who we are in Christ. Does our behavior reflect Christlikeness?

CLOSE WITH PRAYER. Address any issues or needs expressed during discussion.

WEEK THREE

Open with prayer and invite the Holy Spirit into your meeting.

DISCUSSION QUESTIONS
When you think of Jesus, what comes to mind?

Did you discover something new about the Holy Spirit as you worked through Lesson 2? If so, please share.

Read out loud Luke 22:31–31 and 1 John 2:1–2. Discuss what Satan does and how Jesus responds.

Based on what you've learned up to this point, have you discovered an area or two or three where Satan has deceived you? Share about this.

Ask if there are any areas where attendees have a consistent struggle, then search out and find verses that can help each other replace Satan's lies with God's truth.

What lesson in this chapter spoke the most to you and why?

DIVING DEEPER (TWO WEEKS PER CHAPTER)
Chose a few questions from the general discussion questions above and supplement them with these or your own.

LESSONS 1–2

Discuss how Jesus fulfills Psalm 23.

Discuss the role of the Holy Spirit in our lives.

LESSONS 3–5

Discuss How Satan works and how we can recognize his deceptions.

Discuss Romans 5:8 and how it speaks to how much God loves us.

CLOSE WITH PRAYER. Address any issues or needs expressed during discussion.

Open with prayer and invite the Holy Spirit into your meeting.

DISCUSSION QUESTIONS
Describe your relationship with God the Father. Jesus the Son. The Holy Spirit. How do you nurture those relationships?

Discuss the "FIVE STEPS FOR RECEIVING FROM GOD" listed in Lesson 2 (page 76).

Discuss what John 15:16 means to each of you.

Discuss Numbers 23:19, what it means to you and how it impacts your faith.

Discuss how reading and studying the Bible and taking action on the Word helps our faith grow.

What lesson in this chapter spoke the most to you and why?

DIVING DEEPER (TWO WEEKS PER CHAPTER)
Chose a few questions from the general discussion questions above and supplement them with these or your own.

LESSONS 1–3

Discuss the three fundamentals of faith listed in Lesson 2: believe it and speak it; receive it; forgive.

Discuss the fact that God doesn't show partiality and how that impacts your faith.

LESSONS 4–5

Share and discuss individual perspectives on what it means to walk by faith.

Ask the group to share how they nurture their faith.

CLOSE WITH PRAYER. Address any issues or needs expressed during discussion.

WEEK FIVE

Open with prayer and invite the Holy Spirit into your meeting.

DISCUSSION QUESTIONS
Discuss the various ways God speaks to us. Refer to specific verses when needed.

How do we come to know God's character?

Can we walk 100% in God's Kingdom but disobey His biblical commands and principles? Discuss.

Discuss all the promises listed in Isaiah 41:10–13.

Are you resting in God or worrying even after you pray? Ask the group to share.

What lesson in this chapter spoke the most to you and why?

DIVING DEEPER (TWO WEEKS PER CHAPTER)
Chose a few questions from the general discussion questions above and supplement them with these or your own.

LESSONS 1–3

Discuss the various ways God speaks to us.

Discuss the Holy Spirit's role in helping us recognize God's voice.

What is your reaction to the word *obey*?

LESSONS 4–5

Discuss verses that can help the group overcome fears they might be experiencing.

Discuss what resting in God brings us.

CLOSE WITH PRAYER. Address any issues or needs expressed during discussion.

WEEK SIX

Open with prayer and invite the Holy Spirit into your meeting.

DISCUSSION QUESTIONS
Discuss what it means to bind and loose. See Matthew 16:19 and 18:18. Review the original language through the use of a concordance or using tools like BlueLetterBible.org to help you.

Discuss the difference between being baptized in the Holy Spirit and being filled with the Holy Spirit. (See Lesson 2)

Discuss speaking in tongues and pray for any who want to receive this gift.

If we didn't have His Word, how could we know what God can and will do for us?

Share, or ask someone from the group to share, something special that stood out to you from the verses from Psalms listed on page 121 (very beginning of Lesson 5).

What lesson in this chapter spoke the most to you and why?

DIVING DEEPER (TWO WEEKS PER CHAPTER)
Chose a few questions from the general discussion questions above and supplement them with these or your own.

LESSONS 1–3

Read out loud Luke 24:49, Acts 1:8, and Ephesians 3:16 and discuss how Holy Spirit empowers us to fulfill God's plan for us.

Do you think that whatever is spoken in the Spirit (in tongues) is in the realm of Isaiah 55:11? Discuss why or why not.

LESSONS 4–5

Read out loud Ephesians 1:17–20 from the New Living Translation (available at BlueLetterBible.org or a phone app), then discuss each verse.

Spend some time praising the Lord. Encourage those who are unaccustomed to raising their hands to God to do so.

CLOSE WITH PRAYER. Address any issues or needs expressed during discussion.

WEEK SEVEN

Open with prayer and invite the Holy Spirit into your meeting.

DISCUSSION QUESTIONS
Read 1 John 2:16. In what three areas does Satan aim his attacks at us? Discuss each.

How does the "belt of truth" affect all the other pieces of our spiritual armor?

Discuss the importance of and how the helmet of salvation functions for us.

Read out loud John 15:7 and discuss what it means to abide in Christ. (See page 138, middle of Lesson 4, for Strong's Concordance definition of abide.)

If we are praying for something, but speaking the opposite to those around us, how does that affect our prayers?

Read out loud Isaiah 54:17 (read it from several translations to gain greater clarity and depth) and discuss how this verse plays out in our lives.

What lesson in this chapter spoke the most to you and why?

DIVING DEEPER (TWO WEEKS PER CHAPTER)
Chose a few questions from the general discussion questions above and supplement them with these or your own.

LESSONS 1-3

Read out loud 2 Corinthians 10:4-5 and discuss how to recognize wrongs thoughts and take them captive.

Discuss the difference between logos (the written Word) and rhema (revelation of the Word) and the part each plays in our spiritual armor. (The written Word is our belt; rhema is our sword.)

LESSONS 4-6

Discuss prayer and dispel any misconceptions that it must be eloquent, long, or uttered only on our knees at our bedside.

God spoke all things into existence. Since we are created in His image, what does that tell us about the power of our words? Discuss.

Read 2 Chronicles 20:1-15 and review the steps King Jehoshaphat took as he faced this battle. Discuss how this applies to us today.

CLOSE WITH PRAYER. Address any issues or needs expressed during discussion.

WEEK EIGHT (OPTIONAL)

Come together to celebrate completion of the study. Share a meal or snacks.

Open with prayer and invite the Holy Spirit into your meeting.

Ask the group what they liked best about the study.

Ask if anyone is willing to share a testimony of how God used the study to bring about change in her/his life.

CLOSE WITH PRAYER, asking particularly for Holy Spirit to continue to teach and lead each individual as they seek to grow more like Christ and unshakable in their faith.

Bonus Posters

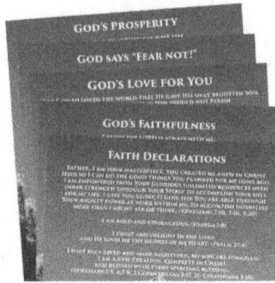

Available with your purchase today are five 8.5 x 11 inch printable posters. Each poster contains topic-specific Bible verses. Posters included are "God's Prosperity," "God Says 'Fear Not!,'" "God's Faithfulness," "God's Love for You," and "Faith Declarations."

Visit DebraLButterfield.com/unshakable-bonus/ to claim your posters.

BIBLIOGRAPHY

The Knowledge of the Holy, A.W. Tozer, HarperSanFrancisco, New York, NY; 1961

Be Ye Transformed, Nancy Missler, The King's Highway Ministries, Inc., Coeur d'Alene, ID; 1996

Dressed to Kill, Rick Renner

http://thectp.org/notes/theworshipingchurch/theworshipingchurch_7.pdf

ADDITIONAL RESOURCES

Kenneth Copeland Ministries, kcm.org

Creflo Dollar Ministries, creflodollarministries.org

John Hagee Ministries, jhm.org

Rick Renner Ministries, renner.org

Books
Dressed to Kill by Rick Renner
Battlefield of the Mind by Joyce Meyer

APPENDIX

Who I am in Christ

I have been justified—completely forgiven and made righteous. (Romans 5:10)

I died with Christ and died to the power of sin's rule over my life. (Romans 6:1-6)

I am free forever from condemnation. (Romans 8:1)

I have been placed into Christ by God's doing. (1 Corinthians 1:30)

I have received the Spirit of God into my life that I might know the things freely given to me by God. (1 Corinthians 2:12)

I have been given the mind of Christ. (1 Corinthians 2:16)

I have been bought with a price; I am not my own; I belong to God. (1 Corinthians 6:19-20)

I have been established, anointed, and sealed by God in Christ, and I have been given the Holy Spirit as a pledge guaranteeing my inheritance to come. (2 Corinthians 1:21; Ephesians 1:13–14)

Since I have died, I no longer live for myself, but for Christ. (2 Corinthians 5:14-15)

I have been made righteous. (2 Corinthians 5:21)

I have been crucified with Christ and it is no longer I who live, but Christ lives in me. The life I am now living is Christ's life. (Galatians 2:20)

I am blessed with every spiritual blessing. (Ephesians 1:3)

I was chosen in Christ before the foundation of the world to be holy and am without blame before Him. (Ephesians 1:4)

I was predestined—determined by God—to be adopted as God's son/daughter. (Ephesians 1:5)

I have been redeemed and forgiven, and I am a recipient of His lavish grace. (Ephesians 2:7)

I have been made alive together with Christ. (Ephesians 2:5)

I have been raised up and seated with Christ in heaven. (Ephesians 2:6)

I have direct access to God through the Spirit. (Ephesians 2:18)

I may approach God with boldness, freedom, and confidence. (Ephesians 3:12)

I have been rescued from the domain of Satan's rule and transferred to the Kingdom of Christ. (Colossians 1:13)

I have been redeemed and forgiven of all my sins. The debt against me has been canceled. (Colossians 1:14)

Christ Himself is in me. (Colossians 1:27)

I am firmly rooted in Christ and am now being built in Him. (Colossians 2:7)

I am a new creation. (2 Corinthians 5:17)

I have been made complete in Christ. (Colossians 2:10)

I have been buried, raised, and made alive with Christ. (Colossians 2:12-13)

I died with Christ and I have been raised up with Christ. My life is now hidden with Christ in God. Christ is now my life. (Colossian 3:1-4)

I have been given a spirit of power, love, and self-discipline. (2 Timothy 1:7)

I have been saved and set apart according to God's doing. (2 Timothy 1:9; Titus 3:5)

Because I am sanctified and am one with the Sanctifier, He is not ashamed to call me brother/sister. (Hebrews 2:11)

I have the right to come boldly before the throne of God to find mercy and grace in time of need. (Hebrews 4:16)

I have been given exceedingly great and precious promises by God and by which I am a partaker of God's divine nature. (2 Peter 1:4)

I am complete in Christ. (Colossians 2:10)

About the Author

Debra L. Butterfield dreamed of being writer since she was a pre-teen. Fulfillment of that dream began when she was forty-five years old and Focus on the Family hired her as a junior copywriter. In 2006, she stepped into the world of free-lance writer. In 2014, she joined CrossRiver Media Group as an editor and is now their editorial director.

She is the author of *Unshakable Faith* Bible study, *7 Cheat Sheets to Cut Editing Costs, Carried by Grace,* and *Mystery on Maple Hill* (a short story ebook) and the compiler and editor of *Abba's Promise* and *Abba's Answers.*

Debra is a US Marine Corps veteran, enjoys the outdoors and, oddly enough, likes the smell of skunks. Like most writers, she loves to read, usually not one book at a time either. She has lived as far west as Hawaii and as far east as Germany and lots of places in between. Now living in Missouri, she has three adult children and two grandchildren.

She blogs about writing at TheMotivationalEditor.com. You can find her author page at DebraLButterfield.com You can also find her at facebook.com/DebraLButterfieldAuthor/.

More Great Books From
CrossRiverMedia.com

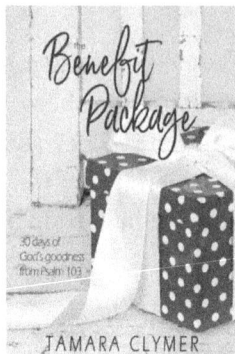

The Benefit Package
Tamara Clymer

Love, redemption, mercy, provision, revelation, and healing...In Psalm 103, David listed just a few of the good things God did for him. His list gives us plenty to be thankful for during tough times. No matter the circumstances or background, God is always full of compassion, generous with His mercy, unfailing in His love, and powerful in healing. When circumstances overwhelm you—unwrap His *Benefit Package* and rediscover God's goodness.

Unbeaten
Lindsey Bell

Does God hear me when I pray? Why isn't He doing anything? Does He even care? Author Lindsey Bell understands the struggle. She searched the Bible for answers to these tough questions. Her studies led her through the stories of biblical figures, big and small. She discovered that while life brings trials, faith brings victory. And when we rely on God for the strength to get us through, we can emerge *Unbeaten*.

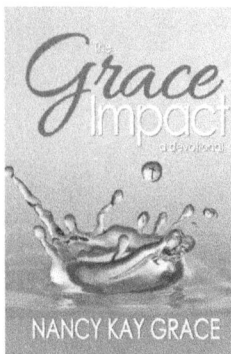

The Grace Impact
Nancy Kay Grace

The promise of grace pulses throughout Scripture. Chapter after chapter, the Bible shows a loving heavenly Father lavishing His grace on us through His Son. In her book, The Grace Impact author Nancy Kay Grace gives us closer glimpse at God's character. His grace covers every detail of life, not just the good things, but the difficult, sad, and complicated things. That knowledge can give us the ability to walk confidently through life knowing God's with us every step of the way.

CROSSRIVER

If you enjoyed this book, will you
consider sharing it with others?

- Please mention the book on Facebook, Twitter, Pinterest, or your blog.
- Recommend this book to your small group, book club, and workplace.
- Head over to Facebook.com/CrossRiverMedia. "Like" the page and post a comment as to what you enjoyed the most.
- Pick up a copy for someone you know who would be challenged or encouraged by the message.
- Write a review on Amazon.com, BN.com or Goodreads. com
- To learn about our latest releases subscribe to our newsletter at CrossRiverMedia.com